T0165719

HANDS ACROSS THE ELBE
THE SOVIET-AMERICAN LINKUP

Edited by Dr. Delbert and Mrs. Donna Philpott

TURNER PUBLISHING COMPANY

TURNER PUBLISHING COMPANY
Publishers of America's History

Hands Across the Elbe Staff:
Dr. Delbert Philpott, Editor
Mrs. Donna Philpott, Editor

Turner Publishing Company's Staff:
Publisher's Coordinator: Pamela Wood
Publisher's Designer: Trevor W. Grantham

This publication was produced using available material. The Publisher regrets it cannot assume liability for errors or omissions.

Library of Congress
Catalog Card No.:   94-61947
ISBN: 978-1-56311-172-3

This publication is a limited edition. Additional copies may be purchased from Turner Publishing Company.

About the Cover Photo . . . *The photograph of the American and Russian Link-up was taken by International News War Correspondent Allan Jackson on April 26, 1945. It is often called the second most famous World War II photo because it symbolized splitting Nazi Germany in half and signaled the end of the war with Germany. It appeared in newspapers around the world in April 1945, and has been in numerous other publications since that time. More details of its background are noted in the articles "Random Thoughts on the Link-up at Torgau - 50 Years Later", by Allan Jackson and "Now When I Look Up at a Bright Dot Moving Across the Night Sky I know the Spirit of the Elbe is Alive and Well", by Delbert E. Philpott.*

CONTINENTAL EDITION — STRASBOURG

YANK
THE ARMY WEEKLY

3 FRANCS **MAY 6 1945** VOL. 1, NO. 41

By the men... for the men in the service

SHOP TALK

DEDICATION

We would like to dedicate this book to all the Veterans who fought for peace and continue to work for peace.

PREFACE

Fifty years have passed since the historic meeting on the Elbe River of the American and Russian soldiers. It is now appropriate to review many of the events and illuminate the effect this historic moment has had on the lives of some of the participants and its continued hope for peace. After reading these contributions and standing beside the old Torgau Bridge, we believe that we can indeed say, "a lot of water has passed under the bridge."

Few events are remembered with such clarity and retain such significance as the Link-up at the Elbe River in 1945. It not only signified the end of Hitler's horrible and senseless war, but real hope for a lasting peace was expressed by the soldiers on all sides. While this understandable wish was side-tracked by the Cold War and intervening events, the dream of peace through understanding was never abandoned by the link-up veterans.

By contacting available participants, a chronology of events has been documented which provides a new perspective for many of the historic milestones from 1945 to the present. While some of the major players are no longer living, attempts to contact their relatives have been made. This has resulted in additional fascinating information.

The editors have striven to accurately present the words of each individual without censorship. Furthermore, we want to point out that incidents and reflections in the stories represent those of the individual authors, retaining the flavor of their memories and effects on their lives. Each experience is unique and historians should know both the good and the bad sides of these experiences. The statement that "War is Hell" is still true. Acts of brutality were committed by all sides which enhance the senselessness of war. The reader should not get the impression that such actions were always condoned by the higher officers. For example, several days after the link-up, three American soldiers were escorting a Russian soldier back to the river after stopping him from raping a German lady. After a Russian officer demanded to know why his soldier was under armed guard and learned the reason, he shot the perpetrator on the spot. By taking the reader on a personal journey with each of the participants, a fresh insight will be realized as events are related. Although it was sometimes necessary to make changes, the editors' intent was to leave the words of the articles as intact as possible.

Yanks Meet Reds - Recollections of U.S. and Soviet Vets from the Link-up in World War II was a significant contribution to history and offered an improved perception of the link-up events and the ultimate hope of peace. Mark Scott's "The Story Behind the Story" provides an intriguing glimpse into the background of *Yanks Meet Reds*. *Hands Across The Elbe* is not only a collection of the experiences of some of these veterans, but also describes how these events touched their lives afterwards. Another difference between the two books is that this work features articles contributed by German Veterans and captivating accounts by journalists of the time. This book aspires to provide insights into the events, hopes and dreams of all those who struggled to bring about peace; and because of experiencing the horrors of war, wanted peace "TO HAVE A CHANCE".

Dr. Delbert E. Philpott and Donna A. Philpott

ACKNOWLEDGMENTS

No one person could have accomplished all the arrangements necessary to produce an historic book covering this many people. Besides the authors of the articles, without whom there would be no book, other people assisted in the preparation. We would like to acknowledge some of them here.

Yanks Meet Reds was the blueprint for *Hands Across The Elbe*. Its editor, Mark C. Scott, provided us with much helpful information and encouragement as well as "The Story Behind the Story". Robert M. Shaw, in addition to contributing both an article and a poem, gave us guidance regarding the publishing world.

Translations from German and Russian: The bilingual talents of native speakers are invaluable. Translations which convey the connotation intended by the author as well as the accuracy of the information are extremely difficult to achieve. This is especially true when one is not proficient in the languages involved; i.e., Russian and German. Without the aid of native speakers, it would have been necessary to rely solely on dictionaries and the mostly literal translations provided by computer programs. Such methods could have resulted not only in inaccurate, but possibly misleading interpretations of the information. We gratefully acknowledge the individuals who provided such invaluable assistance to us.

Mr. H. Schedina, an English teacher in Torgau, not only personally delivered some of the German and Russian stories to us, but also sacrificed several vacation days to assist us in editing some of the German contributions. He was especially knowledgeable with regard to idioms and the identification of several locations. A Leipzig native, Ms. R. Studera, likewise provided translation assistance for the German stories. Her considerable administrative talents, which include making appointments and conducting several interviews on our behalf, are enormously appreciated. Dr. U. Niedersen and Mr. G. Schöne, two gentlemen associated with Torgau's Kulturhaus and "Down By The Riverside" Elbe Days activities each April, helped to collect stories and suggested a general theme for the book.

Without the help of several Russian citizens who were able to relay messages between some of the Russian authors and us, the unreliability of their postal system might have made it impossible to obtain any Russian stories. Dr. L. Serova from Moscow was very helpful in this regard. General A. Olshansky, an Elbe Veteran from Moscow, was instrumental in influencing veterans to contribute their material. Mr. B. Gorbachev, a Russian Veteran from St. Petersburg who saw duty in a different war zone, also delivered messages for us. His daughter, O. Funtak, offered support in obtaining material from Russian Veterans. M. Bukhankova, the daughter of Elbe Veteran L. Zilberberg, whose story is in the book, provided valuable translation assistance.

Photography: Many of the authors made available to us some of their most treasured photographs and other material so that we could include them in the book. Mrs. E. Bräunlich, a Torgau photographer, provided photographs from her extensive collection. Some photographs were obtained from museums and the National Archives. We copied all the photographs loaned to us by the authors. This was primarily done to prevent their loss during shipment to the publishers and for possible use in the potential publication of German and Russian versions of Hands Across The Elbe .

Technology: We would like to thank our amateur radio friends who generously offered their suggestions in converting our computer files to the system specified by the publisher. We are especially grateful to Mr. E. A. Campbell for his able and patient guidance. Without him, it would truly have been a painful process to prepare this book.

THE STARS AND STRIPES

Daily Newspaper of U.S. Armed Forces   in the European Theater of Operations

Russian Lesson
BABY you do SAW
nort-va
filled in hours 3-10

YANKS
MEET
REDS

The American and Russian Armies have met 75 miles south of Berlin to cut Germany in two and seal the final gap between the Eastern and Western Fronts. The linkup, announced simultaneously yesterday in Washington, Moscow and London, was made at 4:40 p. m. Wednesday at Torgau, on the Elbe River. Dispatches from the 12th Army Group indicated that the junction was made when elements of the 273d Reg. of the 1st Army's 69th Inf. Div. met elements of Marshal Koniev's 1st Ukrainian Army.

The long-awaited junction, the greatest of any war in history, was announced in special statements yesterday by President Truman, Prime Minister Churchill and Marshal Stalin.

For days there had been indications that a linkup was imminent or had already taken place. First Army troops had been listening on field radio receivers to Soviet officers giving orders to their troops across the Elbe.

Russian and American troops had been stealing by in soviet cars, and liaison officers of both armies had travelled between the converging lines to exchange plans and instructions.

Other plans for the rendezvous had been made between American and Soviet troops by radio.

3d Enters Austria

7th Slices Munich Gap to 30 Miles

Troops of the 3rd Army yesterday crossed the Austrian frontier at one point and ten miles to the south the Russians had reported the capture west of Vienna. Seventh Army spearheads, exploiting their drive south of the Danube, closed south of the Austrian panhandle near the Swiss border reaching within 30 miles of Austria's

The Germans split by the linkup gave ground as American forces on the Elbe, Patton's armies gaining and driving toward a new junction of American and Soviet armies in the very heart of the southern redoubt.

along the Danube, flank units of the Third Army captured Regensburg on the south bank of the

Soviets Score New Gains North and South of Linkup

While the Moscow victory cannon were booming a 324-gun salute last night to the linkup at Torgau between Russian and American forces, other Soviet troops were gaining fast, to the north and south as the Germans reeled on the Eastern Front from the multiple Russian blows.

Marshal Stalin announced that Marshal Zhukov's 1st White Russian Army, west of Berlin, had captured Spandau, Potsdam and Rathenau, described by Stalin as important defense strongpoints and road junctions. Rathenau, the farthest west, is 18 miles east of the Elbe and of the U.S. 9th Army.

To the north, Marshal Konstantin Rokossovsky's 2d White Russian Army smashed through the defenses of Mecklenburg toward a junction with British troops where have reached the Elbe south of Hamburg.

Rokossovsky's army, which crossed the Oder Thursday, captured Prenzlau and Angermunde yester-

Hitler's Den Wiped Out

Aerial reconnaissance photographs indicate that Allied airmen achieved complete success on Wednesday's unprecedented bombing of Hitler's Berchtesgaden retreat, wiping it out with 12,000-pound concrete-piercing bombs.

Royal Air Force officers said photos showed large numbers of bombs, specially fused to bore deep underground before exploding, had burst squarely in the

Armies Span 2,200 Miles To Make Historic Junction

The two armies had fought their way to a juncture across the entire breadth of Europe – a distance of 2,200 actual miles from Stalingrad on the Volga, where the Germans reached the highwater mark of conquest in the fall of 1942, to the Normandy coast, where the western assault on Fortress Europe was launched last June.

When they met Wednesday on the Elbe Plain, they had between them, broken Hitler's far-flung embattlements and split the remnants of the German armies across the centre of a shrinking corridor reaching from the North Sea coast into the plains of northern Italy.

TABLE OF CONTENTS

BENEATH THE MONUMENT

by Robert M. Shaw
Rifleman, 273rd Regiment, Co. B.,
69th Infantry Division

Fallen soldaten...
In another time you might have been our friend
before you died beneath the monument your victorious ancestors
erected after defeating a great General...
... A Napoleon who was never truly victorious
Nor were soldiers from other times
and from other places

From east and west came generals and footsoldiers,
pilots and sailors, artillerymen and engineers,
doctors and nurses, ministers and priests
all of whom prayed for victory

Yet... who was victorious
Those who returned to Motherland or Fatherland?
But there are no victors.
If only one soldier bleeds to death beneath THE MONUMENT,
Those who lie buried in Otherland?
If only one parent, spouse or child
grieves for the one who died by starvation or by massacre
there is no victory
there is no victor
and THE MONUMENT is a celebration of death
which makes the unborn child cry out:

"Where are the monuments to Peace?"

Please listen to
the heartbeat of the unborn
the laughter
of innocent children and lovers
the music of friendship

Listen to
the boasts of braggarts
the half-truths of politicians
the discord of competitors
the false pride of pseudo-superiors

I am more than you, you are less than I...
Why must ego wait to crush?
Why must wars beg to explode?
It is once more time again
to listen...

...to the laughter of the innocent unborn

May the next hundred years be YOUR Children's Century.

View from the South of the Völkerschlacht-Denkmal monument on the morning of April 20, 1945. (Photo from 69th Inf. Div. pictorial history, Gen. Reinhardt)

BRIDGES OF UNDERSTANDING

by Friedrich Schorlemmer

Building bridges of understanding - which place could be more symbolic than the bridge in Torgau where soldiers of the U.S. Army and the Red Army shook hands and hugged each other? Since 1990, they have been celebrating "Elbe Days" there. Russian and American Army bands play jazz and the peacefully unified Germans enjoy it. On the Elbe meadows, they have a European jazz festival with a political background. I look forward to it every year. I go there, listen to bands from Lithuania and Poland, from Switzerland and Scotland, discuss things, dance, and preach. That's life.

But I also recall how different it was in 1985.

At a meeting of our peace groups in Herzberg in October 1984, I allowed my imagination to be free while we were having coffee and invited those 50 people to come to Torgau. I told them of a big event being planned with Udo Lindenberg and his "Panic Band" performing there. They would drive American and Russian tanks made of cardboard onto the bridge. Crashing into each other, the tanks would break into pieces and eventually Soviet and American musicians would get out and sing pacifist songs. Lots of people would be on the Elbe meadows to see the performance. There would be big tents. Udo would sing on a large stage over the bridge. I would read and explain the U.N. Human Rights Declaration referring to the East-West confrontation as well as to peace between nations in the country. The profit of the entire music performance was to be used to reconstruct this symbolic, but now fragile, bridge.

Some weeks before April 25, 1985, we were informed by the administration of the Halle and Leipzig counties that the GDR state security had reproached and warned the church officials not to plan any provocations which would then have to be stopped by all means available. Church activities should be confined to church rooms only. They said they knew of groups of incitors going from Leipzig to Torgau. In this connection, they also mentioned my name.

How did they know that I was in the group preparing a church service there? We were a group of only 8 people of our provost district and knew that we could trust each other. Why should I be involved in provocations? Then my sister from Herzberg reminded me of my vision during that meeting in Herzberg several months before. (Knud Wollenberger had taken part in it.)

(Ed. note: K. Wollenberger was the husband of a GDR dissident.)

After that plow-making campaign of 1983, they seemed to be prepared for everything with me. (Ed. note: In 1983, on the occasion of the 500th birthday of Martin Luther, Schorlemmer actually DID make a plow from a sword as a demonstration of peace. He made the "beating of swords into plowshares" a symbolic act - not just talking about it.) Even in our group preparing the church service, we argued about how far we could go with our words.

In the morning hours of April 25, 1985, a big show with long and clichéd speeches took place, organized by both the party and the army. In the side streets, we watched young men getting on and off buses.

The ecumenical service in the evening with the Russian Orthodox Bishop "for Berlin and all of Central Europe" had attracted an astonishingly high number of people. We had thought about every word very carefully, and perhaps for the first time after 1945, we talked in public about things which had long been taboo, but never-the-less concerned many people. I quote from a passage which became important again six years later:

"An untold number of people have suffered from Nazi dictatorship, especially during World War II. Here in Torgau alone was a military prison with about 3,000 convicts, four camps of forced labor from Eastern Europe, and a POW camp with about 1,000 prisoners. All of them were really liberated then.

Many Germans experienced these days quite differently as refugees and being pushed around, afraid of the victor's revenge. Strangers in their own country.

Others had to pay the penalty after the end of the war - the guilty as well as the innocent people - in the prison of Torgau, the camp at Mühlberg and elsewhere. Silence lies upon that time (i.e., nobody talks about those times.)

Let us pray: Lord, you promised that the prisoners shall be free and the oppressed be raised up. We beg you, make us free from every kind of obligation. Kyrie eleison."

After the political change, there is a tendency only to speak of Mühlberg and the time after 1945!

The Geneva negotiations on mid-range missiles between Kampelman and Karpow were at a crucial point at that time. We wrote a letter and asked church visitors to join us in signing it. The following day, it was sent as a registered letter to both the American and Soviet Delegations in Geneva. When I asked a U.S. diplomat later whether that letter had reached its destination, he inquired and had to say no. It probably had already been confiscated at the Torgau post office. But it became known, never-the-less, thanks to the "FRANKFURTER RUNDSCHAU" newspaper. They quoted it in full length, but unfortunately with one alteration which they did with good intentions. The last sentence of our letter was in fact, "Please RISK peace". We understood peace as a venture. The editors, however, thought it was a printing error and changed it into "Please DON'T risk peace". (Ed. note: The literal translation is "risk". However, the word "try" conveys the connotation intended in the original text.)

In order to show what the height of common sense among us was at that time, we are reprinting the letter here which was signed by about 100 churchgoers. Everybody had to think about whether he personally could afford to sign it. After all, collecting signatures was illegal.

The title of my speech in Frankfurt on the occasion of being awarded the Peace Prize of the German Bookkeepers' Society in October 1993, resumes this idea of "risking peace".

The East-West confrontation of the Cold War has come to an end. The intercontinental missiles are no longer directed against cities of the former enemy. But peace has not become safe yet.

Now, next to the decrepit bridge of Torgau, a new one has been built and the old one torn down.

Has everything come to an end - is everything beginning again? Peace has to be risked AND can be celebrated. We need to continually remember to keep us from repeating the errors of history.

Peace needs such meetings of people from different nations. Torgau has always been an excellent place for meetings to build bridges of understanding.

(Ed. note: A translation of the letter referred to in Schorlemmer's article is provided below.)

To the U.N. Delegation of the USSR in Geneva, Switzerland
   Attention: Ambassador Victor Karpow
To the U.N. Delegation of the USA in Geneva, Switzerland
   Attention: Ambassador Max Kampelman

Dear Mr. Karpow:
Dear Mr. Kampelman:

Forty years ago today the troops of your two armies met at the Elbe near Torgau. We have gathered today in Torgau's town-church for a peace service to celebrate this occasion, to recall the history of the war and to ask for a peaceful future.

We Germans were your enemies at that time against whom you were allies. Tremendous suffering was put on the nations of the world by Germany. Even though we ourselves were not directly involved in the outrage or already belong to a different generation, we feel a particular guilt out of which results a special obligation to work for peace and understanding. Our country has been split down the middle by a dividing line. We would not be able to survive a military conflict.

You are negotiating in Geneva on behalf of your governments. Whether we will have an increased nuclear arms race or disarmament and whether we will achieve mutual security or would still threaten to destroy each other depends essentially on the results of your talks.

A lot of hope, including ours, rides on your decision.

On this Anniversary, we would like to ask you instantly:

Look with courage and patience for every possible way so that
armament on earth is stopped, armament in space will not be started, and highly destructive weapons will be destroyed.

We are deeply afraid that otherwise, all nations might experience incredible suffering and our countries unintentionally would become uninhabitable deserts. We don't see any reason which could justify the use of massive weapons of destruction. That's why we should not produce and should dismantle weapons that must never be used. Instead, all our efforts should be directed toward eliminating hunger.

We hope and pray for you that your negotiations will be carried out honestly, seriously, and concisely to keep our earth a suitable place for us and future generations.

Please risk peace !

                                        Hans Treu
                                        Hans-Christoph Sens
                                        Friedrich Schorlemmer
                                        Annemarie Wartenburger
                                        Christiane Sens
April 25, 1985
                          People present at the Church Service

---

THE STORY BEHIND THE STORY

by Mark Scott

Several months after the publication of *Yanks Meet Reds*, I had a memorable telephone conversation with former war correspondent Ann Stringer. "There certainly is a story behind this story," Ann told me. "You should write a book about how the book was written!"

Now with the Berlin Wall a thing of the past, Soviet Communism in disgrace, and nuclear missiles being dismantled, most people would not be interested in reading such a book. But Ann was right. The story of how the story was written is an interesting tale.

It involved me trying to secure the cooperation of individuals who traditionally avoided cooperating with each other. American veterans who regarded the Soviets as "Godless Communists" refused to write memoirs for *any* Soviet-American publication. West Germans did not want to cooperate with East Germans. East Germans did not want to cooperate with West Germans, especially with West Berliners. Believing that *Yanks Meet Reds* should be solely a Soviet-American publication, the Soviet publisher did not want German stories included in the book. All parties dreaded that they might somehow be exploited for propaganda purposes, thereby incurring the wrath of patriots back home. Yes, there were many compelling reasons for a veteran of the Meeting at the Elbe *not* to write a story for the book.

Yet despite the suspicions, all the parties agreed that the book was important, if not essential, because at the time they all feared an impending nuclear war. To everyone, the Meeting at the Elbe memorialized the destructiveness and suffering of Total War. To many, it dramatized the belief that people are more important than politics. To Ann Stringer, it proved "it is possible for people to get along." To Buck Kotzebue, it celebrated "that very real feeling of friendship" that had once existed between allies now adversaries. And to Bill Shank, "It was a manifestation of the universal brotherhood which knows neither enemies nor strangers, the religion pronounced in the greatest sermon of all time: 'Our Father.'"

As American editor, I regrettably had to exclude many dramatic stories from the book because they made heroes less heroic. The Soviet publisher did not appreciate the repeated reference to German refugees fleeing *from* the Red Army, nor reports of German families committing suicide in their homes for fear of capture by advancing Soviet troops. Americans would have strongly objected to stories depicting U.S. soldiers as vandals and looters. And no one—American, Soviet, nor German—would have wanted me to include stories detailing their own soldiers' involvement in rape, pillage, or the summary execution of POWs. Had I insisted on including these stories, there would have been no book. Yet had stories such as these been successfully included, *Yanks Meet Reds* would have been much more powerful, a kind of *All Quiet on the Eastern Front*. Such a book would have given readers a greater appreciation of why the Meeting at the Elbe made an indelible impression on those who were there, why fifty years later some of the participants are still moved to tears whenever they recount the link-up.

For it was an anti-war story the veterans wanted told and not forgotten. "Get the story now while everyone is still alive!" Ann Stringer urged me not long before her death. In fact, she was fighting the effects of several strokes when she vividly described to me that April day in Torgau when a Soviet soldier wearing only blue shorts and a cap spotted her and jubilantly shouted, "Bravo, Amerikanski! Bravo, Comrades!" Although Buck Kotzebue was dying of cancer and in great physical pain, he nevertheless struggled to give me details of his own "meeting with the Russians." Joe Polowsky literally carried that story with him to his German grave.

Many of you may agree with Ann Stringer that the Meeting at the Elbe is a continual reminder that people *can* get along. You may believe it symbolizes friendship and human solidarity. You may consider it a memorial to the fifty million men, women, and children who perished in the Second World War. Yet the story behind the story tells me that human beings are intelligent enough to recognize their common interests. In spite of their conflicting ideologies, in spite of their prejudices and hatreds, in spite of their suspicions, they are nevertheless capable of working together to make the world a safer place. This gives us all cause for hope.

Mark Scott
Ojai, California
April 25, 1994

RANDOM THOUGHTS ON THE LINKUP AT TORGAU--50 YEARS LATER

by Allan Jackson, former International News War Correspondent

It is hard for me to believe that nearly 50 years have passed since I took the photo of American and Soviet troops meeting on a broken bridge in the small German town of Torgau on the Elbe River.

The photo was significant because it showed two great armies linking up and cutting the German Army in half. It spelled the end of World War II in Europe. A few weeks later the Germans surrendered and the war correspondents began thinking about: What Next?

Over the years the Link-Up photo became the second best known photo of the war, behind Joe Rosenthal's flag raising on Iwo Jima. Joe and I knew each other before the war when we worked for rival newspapers in the San Francisco Bay Area. We often ran into each other while covering stories for our papers.

We corresponded briefly after the war and were amused that with all the talent covering the war, photos taken by San Francisco Bay Area photographers became the best known. Joe's photo stands alone as a tribute to the fighting spirit of the American fighting men. Mine illustrates the cooperation of the Soviet and American armies that brought an end to the war in Europe.

As the Cold War developed after the end of the war in Europe, my photo of the Link-Up saw less and less use. However, the Soviets made much of it in their propaganda. In recent years I have seen it in national magazines from time to time as an illustration of the cooperation that existed between the super powers as they joined forces to stamp out the Nazi menace that threatened to engulf all Europe.

At the time of the Link-Up (April 1945) those of us at Torgau were impressed by the friendly manner of the Soviet troops. How-

The second of two of Allan Jackson's linkup photos that circulated world-wide. This second photo was taken to get the soldiers from the two sides to look at each other. (Photo by A. Jackson)

Allan Jackson, INS photographer relaxing with Ann Stringer, UP correspondent, by the Ford V-8 confiscated and made into their press car. (Photo provided by A. Jackson)

ever, the Ukrainian Guards division we met with was a far cry from the Soviet troops that fought their way into Berlin. Or were they? We never met those troops as we did the Soviet Guards division at Torgau. These were the "good old boys" of the South. They had hand-me-down equipment and much of it was captured from the Germans.

I took a brief walk back up the road they traveled to reach Torgau and saw beat up trucks and even horse-drawn vehicles. Some of the first contacts our troops made were Russians riding horses. I even saw an old cloth-winged biplane they must have used for observation.

Those of us at the meeting at Torgau were impressed by the friendly manner of the troops. We laughed and sang, drank vodka, called each other "Tovarch" and ate the delicious picnic lunch the Soviet troops provided. We were told that

The Second Division's L-5 observation plane which flew Ann Stringer on the way to cover the linkup at Torgau. (Photo was taken by Allan Jackson while he was a passenger in a similar L-5.)

the Soviets lived off the land and did not haul their own food supplies, as did the American troops. If so, they were living well at the time we met them.

I don't think any of us at Torgau thought that in the years to come those friendly troops would become our number one enemy. However, we should have seen the handwriting on the wall when within two weeks the friendly troops were withdrawn and replaced with NKVD troops. They did not fraternize and put an end to the friendly exchange that had existed with the Ukrainian Guards troops.

It should also be pointed out that we waited about two weeks for the Soviet troops to reach the Elbe river. Our troops could have advanced to Berlin if SHAFE (Supreme Headquarters Allied Forces Europe) had not called a halt. In fact, General Lawton Collins of the Sixth Army Group briefed the correspondents on how he planned to advance on Berlin; something that never happened.

How did I get to Torgau at that moment in history? I had been working with Ann Stringer of United Press, planning on how we would cover the Link-Up when it happened. We decided it could happen over such a wide area we would have to make some arrangement to get there by air.

We had covered the latter stages of the advance across Germany in a battered Ford V8 I had "liberated" in France. We drove to the Second Division HQ where we had friends we made while covering their drive across Germany.

The division G-2 agreed to keep us informed and even offered to fly us to the Link-Up in their L-5 observation planes. Word of the Link-Up reached us late in the afternoon of April 25. Early the next morning we flew into Torgau.

Our experiences in Torgau have been related before. We were the only two American correspondents in Torgau early in the day on April 26. The one exception was Jack Thompson from one of the Chicago papers. We never did know how he got there so early but it did not matter because he did not represent a wire service.

We had finished our coverage and were just leaving when the correspondents from the First Army press camp arrived. Ann took my film and flew to an air field where she caught a ride to Paris on a DC-3. I returned to the Second Division headquarters where I picked up the Ford and drove back to the First Army press camp.

Ann wrote her story on the plane and filed it at the SHAEF army press headquarters at the Scribe Hotel in Paris. She also turned in my film. We both had a clear scoop on the Link-Up story. The next day my photos and her story hit the front pages of newspapers around the world.

Ann went on to cover the war crimes trials in Nurenburg and eventually married a German born American photographer working for the Army. They collaborated on a book about Germany after the war. Ann died a few years ago in New York.

After some peacetime coverage of Southern Germany following V-E Day. I returned to the U.S. and my old newspaper in the San Francisco Bay Area. However, I returned as a writer and covered the city hall, police and courthouse beats. I kept up my interest in photography but never worked at it to make a living.

In 1950, the Oakland Post Enquirer (Hearst) folded and after working briefly for a Vallejo (California) newspaper, I joined the U.S. Department of State as a Foreign Service Officer and for the next 21 years served overseas in many posts as press and information officer. This included a stint as Chief Press Officer for JUSPO (Joint U.S. Press Office) in Vietnam.

The comparison was obvious. In World War II, we were all eager to serve and do what was necessary to get the job done. In Vietnam most of us felt we never should have gotten involved and wished we were someplace else. I still feel it was two years I lost and will never recover.

One of the better things that happened to me at Torgau was meeting a skinny teenage soldier named Del Philpott. Del was so young when he joined the Army that his mother had to sign for him! I talked him into being in my photo and he is the second from the left. Who would believe that he would return to the U.S., resume his education, and eventually end up as a rocket scientist. We met again a few years ago at a 69th Division reunion and have kept in touch ever since.

Perhaps some good did come from the "handshake on the Elbe". Now that the Cold War is behind us we can look forward to 50 years of friendship with the "good old boys" of the Ukraine and all their Russian comrades.

THE FIRST INDICATION . . .

by Iris Carpenter Akers
War Correspondent, Editor

. . . That We Correspondents Had That We Were Getting Near Russian Soldiers Was From German Civilians Running Away From Them

We were on our way from Leipzig and the Mulde River and the narrow roads began to be filled with people. I quote from my book (published just after the war by Houghton-Mifflin) *No Woman's World* :

Filled with as astonishing a collection of humanity in transit as the World has ever seen. A throng of passing refugees, from varying parts of Europe, and in varying stages of wretchedness, had convinced us that there could be nothing new to the picture - until the days when our dispatches began measuring the distance in less than a hundred miles between our own and the Red Armies.

Roads then, as far as the eye could see, became a slowly - oh, so slowly - flowing river of people who had grabbed everything they could stuff into or on to anything that moved, in a desperate try to get out; to get anywhere, just so long as they ended up in the American zones of occupation, rather than the Russian.

Entire populations of towns and villages joined the trek. Families with all their possessions were crammed into farm wagons hastily roofed with straw, or curtains or blankets, looking for all the world like the covered wagons that trekked their way across American prairies. Some of the women and children crowded into dilapidated cars. There was no gas, so their menfolk pushed. Many had only a handcart in which to stuff children, old folks and such worldly possessions as they deemed most precious in starting life all over again. A few had bicycles on which they festooned everything from the baby to cooking pots. And hundreds upon hundreds just walked.

An invasion such as this couldn't be allowed to just flow through our lines. The order had to be made that civilians and German soldiers on the Russian side must stay there. Prisoners and displaced persons were allowed to cross at certain locations, but some heartrending scenes resulted. Our soldiers were terribly upset. "A damn site worse than any battle," they said.

We were in the living room of a little cottage with a small machine propped among the dresser jars when we first contacted the Russians. A voice crackled, "Hello Russian Army. We can hear you if you will acknowledge our transmissions."

The voice belonged to Signal Officer Lieutenant Colonel Walter Given, and there was no acknowledgment; nor to other calls made by specially trained Russian speaking soldiers trying to make contact 24 hours a day.

"Ike", at Supreme Headquarters apparently was as ill-informed as the reporters. There was no knowing just where the merger would occur. Correspondents had their own ideas.

Some thought it best to stay with the First Army press camp in Spa, in Belgium.

There they would be immediately informed of all situations. Others thought it better to be with Divisions. It was all a mess and we began to think we'd still be fighting instead of meeting to make peace.

Wherever they met - no matter what time, day or night, whether with great ceremony or at some remote spot we HAD TO BE THERE. So wherever nights were spent there was only one thing to do with the days. We jeeped frantically over the entire front, checking divisions and praying that we wouldn't be too far from the right place at the right time.

The first meeting of the two forces, when it came finally, as I wrote in my book, "was between a patrol of the 3rd Battalion 273rd Infantry Regiment of the 69th Division, led by First Lieutenant Albert Kotzebue and one cavalry man who directed the patrol to a meeting with General Vladimir Rusakov of the Russian Guards Division."

This, however, was not the story that newspapers headlined or that the 69th briefed reporters to tell. Credit was given to Lt. William D. Robertson of Los Angeles whose lone Jeep, with a corporal and a couple of enlisted men arrived at the river at Torgau a little later that afternoon. Kotzebue's patrol however, had six jeeps and twenty men - a force much easier to explain if questions should be asked.

One of the men in Robertson's solitary jeep told of the first link-up. "We found ourselves at Torgau under fire", he said. "We thought at first it was German but, it was Russian, so we went into one of the stores and found some paint and white paper to make a sort of flag. We climbed the castle tower and dangled this at the Russians and they shot the hell out of it".

The Corporal continued the story. "After a while, they must have gotten our meaning. The shooting stopped. A man came up to us and I said 'Russky'? He said, 'American'? and we went into a clinch..."

Someone else filled in a few details, "We swapped rations and cigarettes. We had the cigarettes. They had the chocolate!"

After that, it was a mad jumble in my recollection. There was the flow of the refugees, the fall of Leipzig and Prague, the German nurse showing us the corpse of Konrad Henlein, Gauleiter and Reichstatthalter of Czechoslovakia, and crying bitterly, "Oh God, what is to become of our country? Of all stupidity, war is the very greatest."

Correspondents careened through woods, doubling back because of broken bridges and cratered roads, to reach the Elbe River and the banks gradually filled. I saw Bill Downs, of Columbia Broadcasting System, *The New York Herald Tribune's* Russell Hill, Cy Peterman and Bill Stoneham of the Chicago papers and a host of others far too numerous to recall. We got boats from our side. The Russians got theirs and rowed to meet us. I was in a boat with Stanley Baron of the London *News Chronicle* , "Mac" MacDonald of *Kemsley* Newspapers and a Russian oarsman as we crossed, with the rest, on our way to Russian Headquarters.

Headquarters was in one of the unpretentious cottages on the river bank. The Russians were ready with a party. And, what a party!

Again from my book;

> There was no doubt about Russian delight at meeting us. In seconds everyone had been offered drinks enough to get drunk on alcohol as everybody was filled with excitement: Russians, in their mud-gray, high-collared uniforms were dancing and singing and

embracing everybody in olive-drab in sight; to say nothing of the spearhead elements of the Russian slave Army who, complete with accordions (looted from a Torgau factory) had gotten into touch with troops even before we did.

I danced, I remember, with a Russian who was taller than any man I have ever seen. Through an interpreter, he wanted to know about life in America but, since I had never been there at that time, I couldn't inform him.

We danced on carpets from the village, laid over the small lawn, with Russian girl soldiers and the wildly celebrating menfolk. Enlisted men shared an equally delirious time across the street.

Luncheon was served, and it was wonderful. Russian women soldiers paraded and greeted guests. General Baklanov, Russian 5th Corps and General Reinhardt of the 69th were both in attendance. It was all delightful and cordial - for one day only.

The next morning we got to the river bank as invited on the previous day by General Baklanov, to be met by guards and orders to stay on our own side of the river. Bill Stoneham shouted across furiously, "We've been invited by General Baklanov. There's been some mistake." All, however, to no avail.

Some of the correspondents had come as far as from the Dutch border, expecting to meet the Russians and go on to Berlin and the final victory. Their feelings can be imagined, at not being allowed even a sight of a Russian Command Post!

With *The Stars and Stripes* finally headlining "Nazi's Quit", we filed our last dispatches from our press camp, finally, in Weimer, Belgium. And had a party!

Typewriters came off copyroom tables, maps were rolled up, jugs borrowed...flowers snapped from German gardens. Don White head of *AP* thought "looting" - even for flowers - ought to stop now that war had stopped. But, nobody paid him any attention.

Some of our members were going back to home base. Some to assignment in Europe.

I was chosen, as the sole British woman, to accompany the First American Army to the Far East. I had a berth on the troopship en route and got as far as the American West Coast.

From there, I was ordered to Washington to reopen the London *Daily* and Sunday *Express* Bureau.

Would I do it all again? No...? Yes...? Maybe? I don't know.

One thing, however, I am sure of — the hope that one day war will be nobody's world instead of the one I, with so many millions of others, lived through.

Iris Carpenter

From a column in the magazine "Picture Show" to assistant to the film correspondent of the London *Daily* and Sunday *Express*, Iris Carpenter became a leading Fleet Street personality.

She married Charles Scruby, son of Basil Scruby, a leading property developer. Charles, who developed Pettswood near London, and Iris had two children - a boy and girl.

When war came her home was bombed, servants dismissed or called up, and children were evacuated. Her husband took part in the rescue of the British Army at Dunkirk. Iris returned to *Fleet Street Express* to cover the Blitz.

The Ministry of Information drafted James McBride, news editor of the *Daily Express*, as the news editor of the Ministry and Iris as his assistant.

When General Eisenhower came to England with American troops, Iris was loaned to them. She met Mrs. Hobby and the first WAAF's. Iris saw the departure for Omaha Beach and landed with the first six women correspondents - the only British one in the group.

When the war with Germany ended, she was assigned to cover the war with Japan. She got as far as the West Coast, but then "The Bomb" was dropped which signaled the end of the war with Japan. Her London editor called saying, "You were only loaned in Europe to the Americans so you can't go with them. You must return to Washington and re-open The 'Express Bureau' there."

Arriving in Washington, she became the Washington editor of the London *Daily* and Sunday *Express* and correspondent for the *Boston Globe*. This subsequently changed to *The Daily Mail*. Then her talents were used on the "Voice of America" and finally with the U.S. Government where she served with her old World War II colleague, Ruth Cowan, of Associated Press.

Her first husband died shortly after World War II ended. She became Iris Carpenter Akers when she subsequently married her second husband. She brought her girl and boy from England and they are in the United States with their own families. She is retired and living near her daughter.

Iris Carpenter enjoying a high ranking officers' banquet in Torgau while obtaining her press releases about the American/Russian link-up. A menu was even printed for this gala celebration. (Photo provided by Eisenhower Museum)

FROM THE ELBE TO
SCHOLARSHIP FLOWS

by Col. Barney Oldfield, USAF (ret.)
Beverly Hills, CA

But for the Elbe linkup of the (then) Soviets and the Americans in April, 1945, University of Nebraska students named Ilia Tchelikidi, Betty Hutchinson, Brett Young and Gleb Evfarestov would never have had the educational assistance of what's called the Mila and Vladimir Kabaidze Award for Innovation and International Business Development.

For those of us who have memories of being somewhere along the Elbe waiting for the Russians, who chose first to show up near Torgau and collide with the U.S. 69th Infantry Division, it was a tense time because when it happened, WW II in Europe would be over.

My Ninth U.S. Army Press Camp had 76 of the angriest and most disappointed war correspondents, and being near them was about like courting a snakebite. They had all bet the Ninth Army would go right on into Berlin, and the rubbled German capital would be their story. Not to be.

General Dwight D. Eisenhower, the Supreme Allied Commander, had looked at the Yalta-agreed-upon post-war sectors assigned the victors. The Elbe put Americans, British and some French troops miles into German geography which Roosevelt, Stalin and Churchill had decided would be administered by the Soviets. The intelligence estimate was that if the Allies plunged on into Berlin, about 200,000 casualties were likely — and all that territory would then have to be handed over to the Soviets, too. "Hold on the line of the Elbe, and wait for the Russians" was the order. It had a certain tidiness about it, would reduce chances of the converging forces inadvertently killing each other.

But war correspondents, like women scorned, when robbed of their perceived front paging, could be unreasonable, and they were. It had been a pleasure for me to be out along the Elbe stringing out photographers to get the photos wherever it was going to be, or however many places the coming together could be lensed. The shuttlecock in all the rumoring as to where it would occur was Major Joe Biroc, a Hollywood studio cameraman with great credits then and an Academy Award or two to come, was one of Lt. Col. George Stevens' great talents, and Stevens had the only "sound on film" capability in the whole European Theater. There was no CNN then, nor portable satellite dishes. We were still in the cinematic Stone Age. "I've been all up and down this whole —damn front," Joe told me, "and everybody says the Russians are going to meet us here. Where their unit is. I don't think anybody knows anything for sure!"

I didn't know it then, but across the Elbe less than 12 miles from where I was, was a Lt. Vladimir Kabaidze, in what the Soviets called a "Strike Battalion". He had been badly wounded three times, had fought at the deepest end of German penetration in Rostov on the Don River, and at Stalingrad, participated in the destruction of Marshal von Paulus' German Sixth Army Group just over the Volga, the chase of the Germans through Kursk, Berlin, and as one half of one percent of Strike Battalion survivors, he was at the Elbe. The American he would meet and remember forever was a Lieutenant Frank Parent from Huntington Beach, California, who had come all the way from

Normandy with the 30th Infantry Division. The only paper they had to write on when they exchanged addresses was a Kabaidze ruble, and a Parent 100-Deutschemark military scrip note.

It was 41 years later in Chicago that Kabaidze seated himself next to me at the National Machine Tools annual convention to which Kabaidze came as a leading Soviet machine tool manufacturer and part of an attending Soviet delegation. He heard my colleagues call me "Colonel", and he always seemed to be near me. KGB, I thought, but even if this was true there was nothing intimidating about that. We had several other encounters with that delegation, and finally, their tour finishing in Cincinnati, he grabbed the interpreter, came over and told her to tell me he had enjoyed our time together, that I had been gracious and friendly, that he hoped we'd meet again in his country. "I'm drawn to you for some reason," he said. It sort of rocked me as his eyes held mine as if trying to fathom why. As my colleagues were going to take me with them on a reciprocal visit to the U.S.S.R., I told him I looked forward to meeting him in Ivanovo, his town.

That was where it happened. Cold, snowy, blowy Ivanovo was and is primarily a textile town, weavers, 16 women to each man, and the machine tool business came there to bring more men and better balance the ratio. There used to be a song, sung by husbands being given a hard time by their wives, the lyrics threatening "Be nice to me, wife, or I'll go to Ivanovo!" Kabaidze was a chance-taker, had only disdain for the Moscow planners, outwitted them and made so much money (which they tapped generously and let him get away with entrepreneurship and even capitalist attitudes and practices). When Mikhail Gorbachev came to power, he named Kabaidze as one of 16 in the whole of the U.S.S.R. who should be looked upon as role models if that country were to be competitive in the future. He even chose Kabaidze to address the Supreme Soviet and criticize the stultifying bureaucracy which was heavy-handed and impeded necessary change. In Ivanovo, he was a BIG man. People came from all over the Soviet land mass to see what Kabaidze was getting away with, so they could point to him as a guide - on when they bent or broke rules.

At a big dinner he hosted that night, he said it was in his remembrances that once before the Americans and the Soviets had engaged in a joint venture which had turned out well — the meeting at the Elbe River in 1945! Why not try again? I held up my hand and asked where he was when the juncture was made — and we had been 12 miles apart! That was it! The 'old soldier' thing, a common dramatic experience, being at history's crossroads. Only a few human beings get into such an exclusive club, the criteria demanding, and the dues, the lives of one's friends and risk of one's own. I told Kabaidze I was sorry he hadn't been with me in Berlin that first day, July 1, 1945, when I'd gone to the bombed out Reichschancellory with another Russian soldier and piddled on Hitler's desk. I said this denied us a footnote in history of the tortured relationship of our two contries as it was the only record of absolute agreement on what was the right thing to do.

It was then that Kabaidze told me about Lt. Frank Parent, how he'd often wondered if he were still alive, and had life treated him well, what a 24 hours of drinking and whooping it up they'd had there at the Elbe.

Without telling him, I began to plot a fantastic surprise, to find Frank Parent, and arrange a confrontation of the two the next time Kabaidze was in the U.S. Parent, it turned out, was a geophysicist, had engaged in resource exploration for more than three decades, was retired and living in Galveston, Texas. And 43 years to the day and

Reunion arranged by Col. Barney Oldfield in Disneyland for Lt. Vladimir Kabaidze and Lt. Frank Parent. Vladimir was in a "strike battalion" fighting his way from the deepest penetration of the Germans to the Elbe River. He became a machine tool manufacturer. Frank was in the 30th Inf. Div., meeting Vladimir on the Elbe River. He became a geophsicist. (Photo provided by Col. Barney Oldfield. Photo was taken on the veranda of City Hall in Disneyland, CA, by a Disneyland photographer. Disneyland Magic Kingdom, Anaheim, CA.)

hour of their first meeting at the Elbe, I had Mickey Mouse bring them together on the veranda of City Hall at Disneyland. I thought Kabaidze, when Parent showed him that old 100-Deutschemark note, was going to have a heart attack. We filmed the whole thing, called the video, AN UNUSUAL MEETING, and indeed it was.

Soviet correspondents for IZVESTIA, the government newspaper, and PRAVDA, the Communist Party's catechism, and the news agency TASS, were all there, but never a word was printed about their get-together, until ...

Until that day in June, more than a month later, when President Ronald Reagan and Nancy were Page One in Moscow with Gorbachev and his Raisa for their summit — and on Page Seven, four columns wide and from top to bottom of the page, there was the story of the Disneyland reunion of two old soldiers of the Elbe elite. It made the point that in people-to-people terms, the Soviets and the Americans had great friendly ties on which even greater future ones could be built.

On my next Soviet trip, some months later, I told Kabaidze I'd be in Moscow and that I had a pleasant surprise for him. He, with his tiny wife, Mila, a wartime nurse who'd attended him in one of his badly wounded hospitalizations, came to the Mezhdunorodnya Hotel. Having made arrangements in advance with the mezzanine video shop to show them AN UNUSUAL MEETING, I took them there, seated Mila, and Vladimir stood beside her and held her hand. The screen came alive. Mila pressed his hand to her heart and began to cry. Kabaidze had tears in his eyes. We had been alone at the beginning of the video, and suddenly the shop was full. He'd been recognized, and they could see it was about him. All Union Radio & Television had a studio in the hotel, and as soon as it was over, we were taken to the studio and the video went border to border — 11 time zones — to the whole of the U.S.S.R. !

When the Mark Scott - Semyon Krasilshchik first edition of YANKS MEET REDS was published in both countries — my story about piddling on Hitler's desk in the Reichschancellory in Berlin — was not deemed proper for the Soviet Novosti Press edition. When Kabaidze heard of their intent to delete, he flew all the way from Ivanovo, came to the offices of Novosti Press, and confronted the editor asking him to reconsider. The editor still said NO, and Kabaidze went out of his door, arms flailing, saying: "Are you saying what he did on Hitler's desk is not also a common bodily function in our country?" but only in the American version is my July 1, 1945, prank in print!

At the University of Nebraska College of Business, they have a Center for Entrepreneurship and Production. My wife and I decided to establish a Mila and Vladimir Kabaidze Award for Innovation and International Business Development — and it has been exciting to see the interest there is not only in the monetary assistance, but the combination of military shared experience and friendship bound up in it. Unknowingly, this was apparently the only time American individuals have created a scholarship named for individual Russian citizens. It somehow seems to match the enormous difference that gathering at the Elbe made in the history of nations by extending an educational lift or hand in a people-to-people way in honor and memory of soldiers and survivors.

That April day in 1988, when Kabaidze and Parent met in Disneyland, Kabaidze told me he had not wanted to come to America at that time. Why? Every year, he said, on or about VE Day's anniversary, he would go to one of the many cemeteries dotting the way from Rostov and Stalingrad to the Elbe. "I stand there", he told me," and I look at those old names and I say to myself, 'Why me? Why was I the one to live on, and they did not? And I feel deeply that if one is spared, there must be some reason and one had better do the best he can with what's to be the rest of his life'." And, of course, the Kabaidzes have done that. Their award will cause scholars every year forever to wonder about them, what extraordinary people they were, as were the deeds in which they participated.

When students go to Russia from the University of Nebraska, the Kabaidzes want to meet and talk with them. It's "living memorialization" in the best sense — monetary assistance with faces and extraordinary lives attached.

How much better could it be? And it will run on as long as the Elbe itself!

Col. Barney Oldfield, USAF (Ret.), was ROTC-commissioned 2nd Lt., Infantry, University of Nebraska, June 6, 1932; became the first newspaperman to become a paratrooper; transferred to the USAF in 1949, did 30 years 3 months and 25 days in uniform; along the way was a press agent at Warner Brothers and had "duty" with Errol Flynn, Ann Sheridan, Jane Wyman, Ronald Reagan, Janis Paige, and a kid named Elizabeth Taylor; was 27 years with Litton Industries and their Director of International Relations, including East/West Trade with the old U.S.S.R. As in the Kabaidze case, his wife, Vada, was one of the original WAACs, which transitioned into the WAC, and she served 24 months in Africa, Sicily and Italy in Communications with Hq 12th Air Force. The Oldfield's have established more than 250 scholarships, the latest being the Nebraska, North and South Dakota Normandy Scholarship Funds honoring the D-Day fallen from those states, initiated on the 50th Anniversary of D-Day, 1994.

FOX TROTS AND BALALAIKAS

by Deborah Kotzebue Kelly

I received a photograph in the mail the other day. Memories came flooding back, memories which that singularly fearful and self-protective (and perhaps, despite the cortical protestions of the civilized self, even primitive) part of my psyche had, until that moment, so doggedly remembered to forget.

A handsome, middle-aged man. An attractive young woman. Each held a picture of a man in uniform, one American, one Russian. I remember those pictures, that day. Elbe Day, 1987. What the photograph does not show is the Kremlin Wall, the Tomb of the Unknown Soldier. The brides and their flowers. The tears.

The woman is me. The good-looking American in the picture I hold is my father, then 2nd Lt. Albert "Buck" Kotzebue, at the cocky age of 22. The memory of this moment, frozen in time and captured in black-and-white outside the Kremlin Wall, hangs surreal as a Dali landscape in a neglected back gallery of my mind. It was taken five weeks after my father's death. Since I took that sudden and unexpected journey to the Soviet Union, I have frequently been asked to write down my memories, yet I have never so much as acknowledged the requests. Something inside was still overwhelmed and unready.

Today, this Easter Sunday, 1994, I will forget to not remember...

Easter Sunday, 1987. I was flying toward Moscow in the belly of an Aeroflot jet. One month to the day after my father had died of cancer, my head was still spinning at the fact that I was the Vice-Chairperson of a delegation of eight Americans invited to visit the USSR. Besides Bruce Robertson, the son of the delegation's Chairman, I was the only delegate who was not a World War II Veteran or a participant in the 1945 Soviet-American Linkup at the Elbe River. And I was definitely the only woman. It all happened so quickly and, knowing that I was there only because my father was not, my thoughts were compellingly drawn back to some of my earliest recollections of him. And of what came to be known by my family as the "Elbe Collection" of family legends.

It seemed that the stories never came from him, yet somehow they were told and told again, or maybe we just osmotically knew them, like ancestral memories. Dad's patrol surprising a lone Russian horseman, knowing that Soviet military units must be nearby. Orders from headquarters to stay within a three-mile radius. The powers-that-be were quite horrified, it seems, at the prospect of an uncontrolled meeting between the two as-yet unintroduced military machines. A blind date on a global scale. What if they didn't like each other?

As the legend has it, my father (honestly, I always thought of him as more a cowboy in camouflage than an honest-to-goodness by-the-book soldier) proceeded to turn off the jeep's radio, ignore orders and follow his nose. Since we Kotzebues have always prided ourselves on our keen and rather prominent olfactory equipment, he quite naturally sniffed out a whole passle of Soviet military types. One problem: they were on one side of a very formidable, spring-engorged German river and he and his men were on the other.

As you might imagine, this was no obstacle for a cowboy and his gang, well-armed as they were with their modern-day versions of six-shooters. They simply used a grenade to blow the chain off a boat moored nearby, paddled across with the butts of their rifles, (I understand this feat of theatrics didn't go quite so smoothly when repeated later for news cameras), and courteously accepted the proffered canteen of vodka. Toasting to the downfall of fascism with what I imagine was a rather mischievous glint in his eye, my father asked to be taken to their leader.

At this point the oft-embellished legend tells of a few glorious hours of ignorant, blissful celebration: fox-trots to the mournful strains of the balalaika, cheek-to-cheek flirtations where language and ethnic origin were no barrier

Deborah Kotzebue Kelly holds a picture of her father taken in 1945, as she poses next to General Olshansky for a photo during her trip to Moscow in 1987. (Photo provided by A. Olshansky)

and in fact only spiced the delirious and innocent belief that all was now right in the world.

Now, once again, it was Elbe Day. In my father's name, I was in Moscow at the Tomb of the Unknown Soldier. Honoring the dead, imploring the living. Trying to bridge the years and fears and bombs that had grown like the cancer that had so recently claimed my father's life. So as we delegates marched with a wreath between us, to the strains of what can only be described as a funeral march in the most heart-wrenching Russian tradition, the images — past, present and only imagined — overwhelmed me. After we laid the wreath on the tomb, General Olshansky, my father's Russian counterpart, kept me on my feet with a firm arm around my waist. But, always the showman, he handed me the picture of my father and pointed me toward the waiting journalists.

Thus, the photograph.

One of the questions I've been asked to answer in this rambling narrative (being a bit of a cowgirl myself, I'm afraid I also tend to follow my own nose), was whether my father had a change of heart about participating in the "Spirit of the Elbe" efforts. I don't believe that hearts change (though they are sometimes prone to break). No, my father merely got his heart out of hock to the pawn-

"Buck" Kotzebue and Gen. A. Olshansky reminiscing on the banks of the Elbe River in Strehla where they met in 1945. (Photo provided by A. Olshansky)

"Buck" Kotzebue with Gen. A. Olshansky in April 1986. (Photo provided by D. Kelly)

brokers of fear. A fear which caused two generations on both sides to numb ourselves to the specter of mass death by vaporization.

Meanwhile, the "official" linkup had taken place and the powers-that-be on both sides were growing more paranoid by the moment. The ordinary, battle-weary unsung heroes might have tears of relief in their eyes as they danced to the death-knell of the "Good War", but a new kind of war, the not-so-Cold-War was being born. And the rest, as they say, is history.

(Except, of course, for my dad. Torn between giving him a medal and giving him hell, his superiors decided to ignore the whole mess. So the only official commendation to adorn the walls of my childhood homes was a Soviet medal, framed on black velvet. The supposed feud over which linkup was the "real" one was never a consideration for my father. Like Buck Rogers, his namesake, he did what he wanted and was perfectly happy to have the adventure and leave the credit to others.)

In spite of the family legends, the monumental impact of that period of history never struck home until I arrived in the Soviet Union. The very much alive memories of twenty million dead. Thousands of villages destroyed. German tanks within sight of the Kremlin, German boots ringing on the floor of the Summer Palace. The 900 days and one million deaths of the siege of Leningrad. Brides on their wedding day bringing flowers to the Tomb of the Unknown Soldier. Pozhaluysta, please, no more killing.

Ultimately, he did break through the fear instilled by American propaganda that he would be a tool of Soviet propaganda, and participated freely and fully. He revisited the Elbe in 1985. He made a passionate plea for reason and peace in Geneva that same year. He got out of the war business, bought a cowboy hat and died with his boots on. In my hopeful moments I like to believe that he made a difference.

So to the men and women who danced on the muddy banks of the Elbe that day, "Na zdorovye" and "Here's lookin' at you". To Buck, I promise, I will remember.

Deborah Kotzebue Kelly
April 3, 1994

THE MEETING ON THE ELBE — ITS PERSONAL AND LARGER MEANINGS

by Igor N. Belousovitch
273rd Regiment, Co. E.,
69th Infantry Division

Before starting to write my contribution for this 50th anniversary edition (evidently, the final one), I re-read several earlier anniversary publications. The one that appeared in 1988 in parallel U.S. and Soviet editions ("Yanks Meet Reds") was by far the best set of recollections thus far in providing fascinating details from witnesses and participants of both sides. What struck me was its narrow focus on the event itself. It was remembered in the spirit of a military unit's reunion long after the war (in a way, it was exactly that), or the reunion of a school graduating class, with much camaraderie and recollection of youth. What was missing was any attempt at reflection or serious effort to place the Elbe link-up in a larger historical perspective, especially relating to the effect it had on subsequent U.S.-Soviet relations during the Cold War period. Had this been attempted, there is little doubt that the rigid differences in political and ideological perception by the two former allies would have precluded a joint edition. Keeping the focus narrow, on the other hand, permitted a limited but thoroughly enjoyable and useful collection of reminiscences.

But unit or class reunions do not normally celebrate a historic event, while the Elbe link-up most assuredly was such an event. Surely, its witnesses and participants should not be required to wait more than fifty years before sharing some serious, personal impressions. Even sensitive government archives get declassified after that kind of time interval.

Now, following the collapse of the Soviet regime and the end of the Cold War, for the first time Americans and Russians have an opportunity to work together not only in seeking, sharing, and discovering the facts affecting their relationship, but in finding larger historical meanings. Hopefully, some of my thoughts will be acceptable to both sides.

Fifty years after an important event, a participant or eye-witness can discuss it either by recalling the event itself, or by describing its results and the role it played in his life. The first way has one serious drawback. The passage of time often erases details and leaves only general impressions. In my case, an account of "how we met the Russians on the Elbe" is not likely to break new ground or provide details not already in the public record. Briefly, I was assigned to Major Craig's patrol because somebody at Headquarters of the 273rd Regiment remembered about a Russian-speaking PFC in Co. "E" who might be useful to have around should Major Craig succeed in establishing contact with the Soviet army.

Aside from acting as interpreter, I also carried in my pocket a small cheap folding camera with a roll of liberated film. The shots I made that day proved to be the only photographic record of the Craig patrol, including its departure from Wurzen after crossing the Mulde River at dawn, encounter with a Soviet cavalry patrol, and finally, arrival at the Elbe and contact with elements of the 58th Guards Division and General Vladimir Rusakov, its division commander. Later, when Major Craig and Captain Fox, an Army historian, realized what I had in that camera, they offered to take the film for processing and printing somewhere up the line. Given its historical value and the hectic conditions at the time, I was surprised and gratified to get my negatives and a set of prints back a few days later.

The Aftermath

In wartime, the events of a single day, no matter how dramatic, tend to disappear into a larger fabric; of battles lasting weeks or months; of victories and defeats; and of policies, negotiations, and decisions. Only a few individual days of the war in Europe survive in the public mind: D-Day in Normandy, the fall of Berlin, V-E Day, and, of course, the link-up of American and Soviet troops on the Elbe that cut Germany in two.

When the war ended and I resumed my studies at the University of California at Berkeley (so rudely interrupted by military service), it seemed to me that soon the Elbe link-up would become little more than a footnote to the war, even though it would always remain with me as a fascinating personal experience. It soon became clear, however, that being an Elbe veteran was going to play a larger role in my life than I ever imagined and would stay with me right up to my obit. It kept surfacing at odd times and in unexpected ways.

Initially, this was the result of efforts by a few Elbe veterans to stay in touch with each other and keep the memory of the event alive. During the early stages of the Cold War this was done with little interest or support from the U.S. government or veteran's organizations. As the years passed, these idealistic and perhaps naive efforts began to attract increasing media and official attention. Why? Because of all the events of the war in Europe, only the Elbe link-up acquired a new and larger meaning during the postwar period in the context of the almost fifty years of the U.S.-Soviet confrontation.

Both superpowers competed for advantage and influence, but they also understood the importance of maintaining all elements of their dangerous relationship in balance. Various types of public information and cultural exchange programs facilitated people-to-people contacts; beyond their propaganda value, such activities played an important role in preventing bilateral relations from deteriorating uncontrollably. In this context, both sides found it useful to invoke the powerful imagery of the wartime alliance and the dramatic link-up of U.S. and Soviet troops as comrades-in-arms. It was, in effect, a way of exorcising the fear of war.

Both sides did it repeatedly. Official U.S. use of the Elbe link-up is perhaps less well known to the American public because the U.S. Information Agency's Russian-language monthly journal *Amerika* is distributed only in the Soviet Union (now Russia) and is by law prohibited from sale or distribution in the

Craig's patrol—first jubilant meeting of the Americans and Russians. (Photo provided by I. Belousovitch)

U.S. The issue of April 1985 (No. 341), for example, featured the well-known wartime photograph of Lt. Bill Robertson and Alexander Silvashko embracing each other following their historic meeting on the half-destroyed bridge across the Elbe. Inside, eight pages of text and pictures were devoted to the 40th anniversary of the link-up. The Elbe theme was used repeatedly on earlier occasions by *Amerika* as well as by Voice of America broadcasts.

Several personal experiences illustrate how being an Elbe veteran has intruded into my life in unexpected and even bizarre ways, making me feel like a member of an esoteric brotherhood.

Summer in Maine

For more than twenty-five years, summer for our family has meant summer in Maine; specifically, in our small house on an island off the coast of Maine. Islesford on Little Cranberry island is a village of lobstermen and summer cottages connected to the outside world by a mailboat that ferries passengers, groceries, and mail — but no cars. Life there tends to be leisurely and, well, insular.

In a community where everybody knows each other — often over a period of several generations — our circle of friends includes long-time summer residents George Peck and his wife Annie. One summer, years ago, my wife learned during a casual conversation that George was a POW in Germany and had been liberated in the area and at the time when the U.S.-Soviet link-up on the Elbe took place. Major Craig's patrol did drive through a POW camp where the POW's were already in charge. They cheered us wildly and surrounded our jeeps. That summer, George and I decided it was a small world and hoisted a glass to our proximity, if not actual meeting, that day in April 1945.

Years later, when Bill Robertson was passing through the Washington, D.C. area and stopped by for a visit and dinner, Maria mentioned our island friend as an example of a far-fetched coincidence. At the mention of George Peck's name, Bill's reaction was one of incredulity. It turned out that George had been with him when the two of them crawled across the half-destroyed bridge across the Elbe and made the celebrated link-up with Soviet soldiers precariously on the steel trestles halfway across. Bill had not seen George Peck and had had no contact with him since that memorable day. Then and there in our living room, my wife dialed George's number and handed Bill the phone. Across the time and the distance, they beat the mathematical odds and reestablished contact.

Americans waiting in the early morning mist to cross the Elbe River. (Photo provided by I. Belousovitch)

30th Anniversary of WWII

Judging by media attention to the subject beginning early in 1975, it was clear that the Soviet regime intended to celebrate the 30th anniversary of their victory in WWII as a major political event. Wartime allies were invited to send both official delegations and groups of war veterans.

I remember receiving a call at the State Department from the reception desk at the main entrance that I had a visitor. It turned out to be Yulian Semyonov, a Soviet writer well known to readers in the U.S.S.R. for his spy novels featuring the Soviet equivalent of James Bond. His purpose, he explained, was to make sure that the U.S. veterans' delegation included participants of the Elbe link-up, and that he had obtained my name "from the Pentagon." Was I interested? I most assuredly was, although his role as emissary did make me feel like a minor character from one of his novels. Subsequently, State not only cleared my attendance of the Soviet celebration, but gave me a second hat to wear by assigning me as escort officer to the veterans' group. It meant that I traveled with a diplomatic passport and the Department paid my air fare. (On such occasions, the invited guests usually incur the costs of travel to destination, while the hosts pick up the expenses inside the country.)

We arrived in Moscow in early May 1975, for about ten days of scheduled activities and travel as guests of the Soviet Veterans Committee. Our group consisted of seven members and two wives, with Bill Robertson and myself as the group's two Elbe vets. In addition to the delegates representing World War II allies, Moscow also invited assorted "anti-fascist resistance fighters" and third world radicals, including groups and countries having little or no connection with the war; they included North Vietnam, Syria, Ethiopia, PLO, and many others.

Celebrating the victory of a wartime alliance during the Cold War required Soviet authorities to tread carefully through conflicting ideological, political and propaganda requirements. For example, the Soviet press toned down its own anti-Western propaganda but did publicize statements by the radical third-world delegates. U.S. and other Western veterans were provided an adequate opportunity to

Both sides explaining their positions on a map. (Photo provided by I. Belousovitch)

make public statements. Their presence and remarks, however, were not emphasized in Soviet press coverage. In all other respects, our group received absolutely first class treatment by the Soviet Veterans Committee and other officials, including accommodations, food, activities, and attention to special requests.

Some fifteen foreign groups, including our own, spent three days in Volgograd (formerly Stalingrad). On the second day, the Soviets produced a veteran of the Elbe link-up. Alexander Vakulin was now a Pro-

Russian Commander General Vladimir Rusakov, 58th Guards Division. (Photo provided by I. Belousovitch)

fessor of Forestry at an agricultural institute in Volgograd. We did not remember him personally, but his recollection of places, people and events unquestionably made him the genuine article. I asked him about General Vladimir Rusakov, the CG of the 58th Guards Division, whom we met on the Elbe embankment after being ferried across the river. Vakulin's answer struck me as cryptic: "He is no longer with us," repeated twice for emphasis. The Russian phrase he used was unusual in that it suggested Vakulin knew that Rusakov was no longer alive but did not wish to get into the details. I was about to ask whether Rusakov came to a bad end as a victim of the political system, but we were interrupted and the opportunity was lost. Rusakov, so far as I am aware, has not participated in any of the postwar contacts and reunions between veterans of both sides. Perhaps some reader of these lines who knows can throw light on his fate.

In Volgograd, the table assigned the Americans in the hotel dining room was longer than the others because of the large size of the group, but its location resembled that of a head table. All tables had flags identifying the nationality of each group. An incident on the second day at dinner, however, may have gone beyond what was intended in singling out the Americans for favored treatment. After a full day's activity, a parched member of the group wondered whether it was possible to order a beer. Unaccountably, the meals until then did not include alcohol. Our two interpreters held a hurried consultation with a waitress, who thereupon produced two bottles of champagne. The result was as spectacular as it was unplanned. Every eye in the room focused enviously on the U.S. table and one could feel the unspoken thought: "Why do the Americans rate champagne and we don't?" The effect was heightened when one cork popped loudly and sailed across the dining room just past the nose of a Romanian general. At subsequent meals everybody received beer or wine.

An open-air "mass meeting", scheduled on short notice, took place before a captive audience of Komsomol members and a crowd of passers-by totaling about 400. Bill Robertson was given the favored position first guest speaker, and his appearance was easily the highlight of the meeting. In a talk exactly appropriate to the occasion, he paid tribute to the defenders of Stalingrad, described the link-up on the Elbe, noted the contribution of all the allies to a joint victory, and concluded by making a dramatic analogy between the slow, painful progress of American and Soviet soldiers across a damaged bridge across the Elbe toward a historic meeting as wartime allies, and the approaching link-up of Apollo and Soyuz in space symbolizing U.S.-Soviet collaboration in a period of détente and peace.

A story about the veterans' visit in the local Volgograd paper featured a photograph of an American and a Canadian sharing the honor of carrying a wreath to the eternal flame at the memorial in the central square of the city (the caption: "A group of foreign war veterans in Volgograd"). The accompanying story carried extensive quotations from speeches by the mayor and delegates from East Berlin and Romania, but did not refer to the presence of Western veterans.

This account would not be complete without a mention of the gala meeting in the Kremlin's Palace of Congresses on May 8 to celebrate the 30th Anniversary of Victory. It was organized as a major political event in the typical style and format of Communist Party celebrations. The expertly designed stage setting conveyed a sense of Soviet power and might. The hall was filled to capacity with the Soviet elite and invited foreign guests (we were sitting in the far right-rear).

Leonid Brezhnev delivered the keynote address to the Soviet people, with the political, military and government leadership deployed on the stage. Soviet citizens and western Soviet-watchers alike who were obliged in those days to read leadership speeches will understand what a dreary job it was to digest their rhetoric in order to discover the one or two sentences that contained something new, useful, or halfway interesting. I was surprised, therefore, to hear perhaps the best speech Brezhnev ever delivered. He had experienced the war himself and had witnessed the trials of the country and its people; to his credit, this time Brezhnev spoke simply, sincerely, and from the heart, with a minimum of ideological bombast.

Compared to previous celebrations of VE-Day, the 30th seemed to be treated as a very special occasion. Perhaps it was the cumulative effect of détente policies, the success of the socialist cause in Southeast Asia, and a sense that the country had finally turned a corner. The real reason, however, could be observed in the upstairs buffet hall during the intermission at a concert following the political meeting. Hundreds of aging generals and other high ranking veterans were parading in dress uniforms with gold epaulets and chests of decorations, and accompanied by their wives in evening dress. It was the wartime generation at the zenith of its power and achievement and claiming its due for winning the war and bringing the country a measure of peace and stability. As one Soviet observed to a member of our group, "The 30th is their last chance to celebrate a good round anniversary. Soon they will be too old, and then they will be gone." That was twenty years ago and the prediction has been fulfilled. It is now time for wartime privates and lieutenants to occupy center stage in celebrating the 50th.

Moscow II

Less than a year after the 30th anniversary I was back in Moscow, this time on a two year tour of duty with the American Embassy as the First Secretary of the Political Section. As far as the authorities were concerned, my status had changed from honored guest to adversary. Still, diplomats assigned to Moscow enjoyed privileges and advantages that Soviet citizens could only dream about. Those two years were undoubtedly the most fascinating of my life. What also came as part of the package was a level of surveillance that required psychological and practical adjustments in one's lifestyle. Whether surveillance developed into outright harassment depended in large measure on whether an individual holder of a diplomatic passport engaged in activities that displeased Soviet authorities, but it also reflected the state of bilateral relations.

My Embassy duties included reporting on political dissidents and religious activists. This could not be done without actually meeting these courageous people and socializing with them on a regular basis. The authorities' unfriendly interest in what I was doing was therefore understandable.

Early in 1976, two unconnected events led to an incident where the Elbe linkup was suddenly remembered and resurrected by the KGB. On Embassy instructions, I attempted to attend the trial of a human rights activist. The attempt did not succeed because the militia stationed outside the courthouse did not permit anyone to come in; they claimed that the courtroom was already full. Much later, I learned that they spoke the truth. The court had been packed with regime supporters during the night; the authorities even brought in a field kitchen to feed them.

At about the same time, Moscow became upset and expressed outrage over the fact that Jewish activists in New York City began to harass Soviet diplomats assigned to the UN. There were instances of shots being fired through windows of Soviet residences. The Soviet press gave prominent coverage to such incidents and even suggested that American diplomats in Moscow could feel the wrath of outraged Soviet citizens, especially in the event of Soviet casualties in New York. Some relatively minor harassment of American diplomats did occur, including, I believe, a tire slashing. The one that remains most clearly in my mind, down to the last detail, is the one I experienced personally.

Russian soldiers from different branches; the one with his hand in his coat is from the cavalry. (Photo provided by I. Belousovitch)

Igor Belousovitch (soldier with the mustache) translating. (Photo provided by A. Olshansky)

One day I was leaving a large apartment complex reserved exclusively for the use of foreign residents in Moscow. The practice of maintaining "foreign ghettos" simplified surveillance and tended to discourage social contacts between foreigners and Soviet citizens. Such compounds were guarded by a militia man who kept track of comings and goings by residents and visitors alike. A pair of American journalists were with me, but for some reason they were delayed at the entrance and I walked out to the street

(L to R): Bill Robertson, a Russian veteran, and Igor Belousovitch. (Photo provided by I. Belousovitch)

alone. Almost immediately, three tough looking men surrounded me and one of them began what sounded like a prepared harangue. He first half-asked, half-stated my status as an American diplomat, and when I confirmed it, he launched into an emotional tirade about the dangers Soviet diplomats were experiencing in New York. He claimed that a relative of his — a young woman — was assigned in New York and screamed that if anything happened to her, he would retaliate in kind. "How would you like to be shot at in Moscow?" he asked rhetorically at one point. His story about having a relative in New York did not sound convincing, but I did express agreement that violence against diplomats anytime anywhere was uncivilized behavior. It seemed clear the three goons intended to keep me there for a while but were under instructions not to lay a finger on me. I took a professional interest in their performance, but to be on the safe side, I positioned myself so that my two friends might see me wagging my fingers at them behind my back and realize that something out of the ordinary was going on. This is exactly what did happen; one of them even had the presence of mind to photograph the scene. It appeared in the Baltimore Sun with a brief story headlined "U.S. Embassy official threatened by three Russians." The clipping is yellowing in my "Moscow File" to this day.

The reason this incident belongs here was provided by the head goon's concluding remark when the three realized that they were under observation. I can remember his words verbatim: "It's a shame that relations between our two countries have come to this. After all, we were allies once, we fought together, and we even met each other as friends at the link-up of our armies on the Elbe." The tone and stress of his words left absolutely no doubt in my mind that he had been well briefed before waylaying me outside that apartment complex on Kutuzovsky Prospekt in the center of Moscow. It was convincing evidence that the KGB file on me was complete and well-maintained. The irony of it all was, that those words, if separated from the source, were valid and right on target. No Elbe veteran, regardless of his uniform, could dispute them.

This account of the role the link-up played in my life does not, it seems to me, end with a final episode that is inappropriate to the spirit of the 50th anniversary. Quite the contrary, for a hyphenated Russian-American with a foot in each culture (and whose father was a pilot in the Russian Air Force during world War I), my life has mirrored the rocky course of US/Soviet relations from the Elbe to the collapse of communism. The U.S. and Russia are now entering a new historic period — one more compatible with my own roots. Thus, the approaching 50th Anniversary of the Elbe meeting will bring me around full circle and take place under circumstances that would have been inconceivable two or three years earlier.

OUR PATROL MEETS THE RUSSIANS

by Lt. Bill Robertson
273rd Regiment, 1st Battalion S-2, Intelligence Officer
69th Infantry Division

This story was previously published in "Yanks Meet Reds", edited by Mark Scott and Semyon Krasilshchik, 1988.

My regiment, the 273rd, reached the Mulde River on about April 20. Every GI knew that the Russians were headed in our direction. We knew the ultimate defeat of Nazi Germany was now certain. But when that would happen, how many of us would survive - these were the pressing questions.

Our orders were to stop at the Mulde. No reconnaissance missions were to be made east of the river. Higher authority then decided that American patrols could go east of the Mulde, but no farther than five miles.

I was a Second Lt., S-2 (Reconnaissance) officer of our battalion. I commanded a small squad. Our regiment was bivouacked on the Mulde just across from the town of Wurzen. On April 24, the Bürgermeister crossed to the west bank of the river and surrendered to us. We subsequently moved into Wurzen. My own squad was very busy that night setting up a POW enclosure and checking the area.

By that time, the possibility of meeting the Soviet army had become the sole topic of conversation. All of us were filled with curiosity and anticipation. We wondered what the Russians were doing. Who were they? We knew that they had fought all the way from Stalingrad, from Moscow, that they were tough soldiers. But what were they *really* like? How did they act? Were they friendly or not? All we knew was that they were in front of us - out there somewhere. And we realized that it would be a great honor for the Sixty-ninth Division to be the first unit of the Western front to link up with the Eastern front.

Soon after we entered Wurzen, we discovered a *stalag* (POW camp) just four miles east of the town. Some four thousand ex-POWs straggled in from the camp. Although weak and emaciated, they greeted us with joy shining in their eyes. I was impressed by how much they personified the global aspect of the war. Some had been captured in the North African Campaign. Many were Russians, Poles, Frenchmen, Englishmen, Canadians, Indians, Australians, as well as Americans. Their happiness was indescribable - their eyes followed us as if they couldn't get enough.

The liberated POWs entering Wurzen were soon joined by hundreds of refugees and forced laborers newly freed. There were Poles, Serbs, Czechs, Frenchmen, and other nationalities. Growing numbers of German civilians began arriving on foot, on bicycles, pushing or pulling carts piled high with belongings.

Even though the morning of April 25 was clear, our own situation was not. The Sixty-ninth was setting up tents and field kitchens on the west bank of the Mulde for the ex-POW's and the refugees. German soldiers began surrendering, entering the town in both small and large groups. The crew of a self-propelled 88 millimeter gun mounted on a Panther tank chassis surrendered the weapon to us intact.

Robertson's Patrol. (L to R): Frank Huff, James McDonnell, Bill Robertson and Paul Staub. (Photo provided by P. Staub)

On that morning, I was given a mission by Battalion Headquarters. My instructions were to survey the roads leading into Wurzen to get a rough idea of how many refugees were coming into town. This would enable the Sixty-ninth to make adequate provision for food and shelter. I was further instructed to plan and guard POW enclosures. I picked three men of our Recon section: Cpl. James McDonnell of Peabody, Massachusetts; Pfc. Frank Huff of Washington, Virginia; and Pfc. Paul Staub of the Bronx, New York (Paul spoke German).

The four of us got into a jeep, equipped with a machine gun. But we had neither flares nor a radio. The patrol drove east a couple of miles, saw only a few refugees, and urged them on to Wurzen. We returned to town and at about 10:00 A.M. took another road leading northeast. On this road, we found many refugees whom we again urged to hurry along. We continued to move up the road.

This, then, was the beginning of the patrol that eventually ended up some twenty miles away in Torgau, the patrol which was the second one to contact the Soviet army. When we first left Wurzen, we had no intention of going to Torgau, located quite a distance from us in enemy territory. We had no intention of meeting the Russians. Although armed with a machine gun, we were only one jeep strong - certainly no "motorized patrol".

Driving northeast, the four of us accepted the surrender of a German rifle company of about three hundred men plus officers. I had them stack their rifles and break the stocks. We confiscated their side arms and wrote out a "safe-conduct" pass to Wurzen. We then chased and stopped a German staff car, found it full of medical officers, and sent them back to Wurzen.

The patrol proceeded carefully because I felt that at some point we would encounter rear-echelon German troops - a quartermaster supply depot, field hospital, kitchens, or whatever. We captured two SS men who offered minor resistance, disarmed them, and seated them on the hood of the jeep.

Nearing Torgau, the patrol came upon a small group of English POWs who had escaped from the town and were making their way for the American lines. They told us of some wounded Yanks in a Torgau prison camp. At that point, I decided to continue to Torgau if we could. Up until then, we had encountered no fire except for shots from the SS men who now sat sullenly on the hood of the jeep.

Reinactment of the flag being waved from Hartenfels Castle as a signal to the Russians. (Photo by E. Bräunlich, Torgau, Germany)

The Russians' view of the flag waving from Hartenfels Castle (reinactment). The flag was actually waved from a window one floor higher than in the reinactment. However, the upper staircase is now considered unsafe. (Photo by E. Bräunlich, Torgau, Germany)

Approaching Torgau, we saw smoke coming from a few fires presumably caused by a previous Russian artillery barrage. We reconnoitered the southern outskirts of the town. The four of us now felt quite exposed as we had no means of identification except our uniforms. We didn't have any green flares - the prearranged signal of the Americans to the Russians. So we confiscated a white bed sheet from a German civilian we met on the road, tore out about a five-by-eight foot section, tied it to a stick, rolled it up, and tossed it into the back of the jeep. We thought the Russians might not shoot at us if we met them waving a white flag.

When our patrol reached Torgau at 1:30 P.M., it was a ghost town. I don't believe I saw more than forty German civilians the whole time we were there. In Torgau, we came across the small prison camp at Fort Zinna the Tommies had told us about. It held about forty men, all sentenced to death for espionage. We found two wounded GI's who had been captured only a few days earlier. They were being treated by a Yugoslav doctor. We promised help soon.

Small-arms fire sounded to the east, toward the Elbe. Leaving the two SS men at the prison camp, we drove in the direction of the firing. Our patrol soon met a German civilian who told Paul that the Soviet army was on the other side of the river.

We decided to attempt contact. The time was about 2:00 P.M.

The patrol then encountered some sniper fire in town. We left the jeep, spread out, and detoured around the snipers. By now, the two Americans from the prison camp had joined us. We were a patrol of six.

Because we were planning to contact the Russians who were on the other side of the Elbe, I felt we needed better identification. The six of us broke into the first drug store (apothecary) we saw and found some colored powders - red and blue. We mixed the powders with water, and painted our bed sheet with five horizontal red strips and a field of blue in the upper left corner. The time was 3:00 P.M.

We moved cautiously toward the river. I looked for some tall building or tower from which to wave the flag. Then we saw Hartenfels Castle. It had a magnificent tower very close to the west bank of the Elbe.

The castle had one entrance through a walled courtyard. I went in with Jim McDonnell, Paul Staub, and Ensign George Peck - one of the two liberated American POW's. I left Frank Huff and the other ex-POW with the jeep.

The four of us climbed the circular staircase inside the tower. Leaving the three men on the upper landing, I crawled out at roof level, waved the flag so that the Russians could see it, and began shouting "Amerikanski" and "Tovarisch." The time was about 3:30.

The firing stopped.

Russian soldiers were about five to six hundred yards away - across the river, then some two hundred yards beyond on a sloping grass embankment. They were moving about in the cover of trees at the edge of some woods.

They shouted. I could not understand.

I shouted. They could not understand.

They then fired two *green* flares (not *red*!). I couldn't respond, since we didn't have any flares. They then opened fire again, this time not just at the tower, but at the whole town as well. While this was going on, German snipers were firing at me from the rear.

Broken bridge in Torgau with Nikolai Andreyev, Bill Robertson, George Peck and Frank Huff following. (Photo by P. Staub)

I then waved our American flag, trying to stay under cover as much as possible. I shouted *"Amerikanski"* and *"Tovarisch"* over and over, explaining in English that we were an American patrol.

They ceased firing and started shouting again. I hung the flag pole out of the tower at a right angle so that they could easily see the stripes. By this time, I had sent the jeep back to the prison camp to find a Russian POW who could speak German.

The Russians resumed firing. This time, though, an anti-tank gun coughed from the left side of the woods (I could see the smoke). The round hit the tower about five to six feet from me.

Again, they stopped firing.

The jeep brought a liberated Russian POW from the prison camp. Paul hurriedly explained to him in German what to tell his countrymen across the river. The Russian leaned out of the tower and shouted a few sentences.

All firing ceased.

A small group of Russians soldiers started walking toward the river bank.

We left the tower, ran through the courtyard, and raced to the river. A road bridge stood near the castle. It had been blown up, probably by the retreating German army. Although the girders were bent and twisted, one of them was still above water level. We could see no boats on our side of the Elbe.

I started for the bridge, but the liberated Russian POW got there first. He started across the girder. A Russian soldier on the east bank began crawling on the girder toward us. Following the Russian POW, I climbed, then slid along the girder. Right behind me were Ensign Peck and Frank Huff. The rest of the patrol remained with the jeep. Paul was even taking pictures of us.

The POW met the soldier, passed him, and continued to the east bank while his countryman continued toward us. About halfway across the Elbe, the Russian soldier and I slid down a limb of a huge "V" formed by the bent girder. The symbolism is interesting, since "V" was the sign for Victory. But we didn't think of that at the time.

The Russian was Sgt. Nikolai Andreyev. We shook hands and carefully pounded each other on the shoulder, trying not to fall into the swift current below. The time was four o'clock.

The Russian continued moving along the girder to the west bank. We continued to the east, where we were met by soldiers greeting us with happy yells. More soldiers were arriving by the minute.

The time was 4:45. We three Americans were standing with the Russians on the river bank laughing, shouting, pounding each other on the back, shaking hands with everyone. Frank, George, and I were shouting in English, our hosts in Russian. Neither understood the other's words, but the commonalty of feeling was unmistakable. We were all soldiers, comrades in arms. We had vanquished a common enemy. The war was over, peace was near. All of us would live for another hour, another day.

The celebration continued as more Russians arrived. One produced a box of captured rations - sardines, biscuits, canned meat, chocolate. Wine and schnapps appeared. We toasted each other. We toasted the end of the war. We toasted the United States, the Soviet Union, and our Allies. We toasted our commanders and national leaders.

Pfc. Frank Huff in front of the East-West sign, Torgau, Germany, 1945. (Photo from May 1945 issue, Yank *magazine)*

We gazed at each other with open curiosity. The Russian soldiers seemed quite young, but I guess we were too. They looked like any other combat soldier I'd ever seen, but were cleaner than many. They wore their decorations on their combat uniforms, but didn't wear steel helmets - I don't know why. Several had continued fighting at the front in spite of bandages on their wounds. I was surprised to see such a motley group of pleasant-faced, jolly fellows. We traded souvenirs such as cap ornaments and insignia. I traded wrist watches with a Russian captain who had been wounded five times since Stalingrad. One soldier gave me his gold wedding band.

A Russian major who spoke English then arrived. I suggested we should make arrangements for our respective regimental and division commanders to meet at Torgau the fol-

2nd Lt. William D. Robertson in 1945. (Photo provided by W. D. Robertson)

lowing day at 10:00 A.M. I told him I had to return to our lines. The Major informed me that our patrol had made contact with elements of the Fifty-eighth "Garde" Division of the First Ukrainian Army, commanded by Marshal Konyev.

"Garde" meant that it was a "crack" division cited for bravery in the Battle of Stalingrad.

It was getting late, and I wanted to return to Wurzen before dark. I asked for a liaison group to go with us. Four Russians volunteered. They were Maj. Anafim Larionov, Capt. Vasily Nyeda, Lt. Alexander Silvashko (commander of the platoon at the bridge), and Sgt. Nikolai Andreyev, whom I had met first on the Torgau bridge.

At five o'clock, we re-crossed the Elbe in a racing shell the Russians had found. The eight of us climbed into the jeep and retraced our route. By dusk, we had arrived without incident in Wurzen. At First Battalion HQ, there was more hand-shaking, celebrating, and toasting when it was announced that these were Russian troops, that a link-up had occurred. Photographers were there taking pictures of all of us standing on the steps of the CP.

Suddenly a shot rang out.

A German civilian who had been standing nearby fell to the ground - the top of his head blown off. As blood spurted from the severed carotid arteries, he lay on the sidewalk kicking.

What had happened? We were told that he had been picked up earlier on sus-picion of being a leader of the Werewolf organization and of serving as a prison guard at Fort Zinna. He had not as yet been checked by his American captors. But when he saw the four Russians at the CP, he thought his time had come. As every-one was celebrating, he had grabbed an M-1 from the shoulder of a GI, put the muzzle under his chin, and pulled the trigger.

Not long after this incident, we proceeded to Regimental CP at Trebsen. Regi-ment had already been notified of the link-up. Col. Charles Adams, commander of the 273rd, welcomed the Russian delegation. The reception for my own patrol was a lot less certain, since we had ventured well beyond the five-mile limit. Although we didn't know it at the time, Col. Adams had two other patrols out beyond the limit. The Colonel had already been chewed out at Division by Gen. Reinhardt, commander of the 69th.

A much larger party then joined us as we drove to Division HQ at Naunhof. Gen. Reinhardt welcomed the Russians, but ordered the Robertson Patrol to be locked up in the G-3's office. There was talk of court-martialing us, since we had dis-obeyed orders by going far beyond the five-mile limit. We were in hot water.

But the Power and Presence of the Press are remarkable. Word had gotten around the First Army's Press Camp that the Sixty-ninth Division, at the leading edge of the First Army's lines, might soon make contact with the Russian front. Correspon-dents and news photographers were thick around Division HQ. They *knew* some-thing was happening.

Reinhardt notified Gen. Huebner of V Corps of our link-up. Gen. Huebner berated Gen. Reinhardt, then notified Gen. Hodges of the First Army. Gen. Hodges was awakened at about midnight with the report that the Robertson Patrol had met the Russians and that a Russian delegation was right then at Division CP.

What was Gen. Hodge's reaction? He said he was "delighted" with the news. He told Gen. Huebner to *congratulate* Gen. Reinhardt. All was forgiven.

The Robertson Patrol and the Russians were then introduced to a mob of report-ers. The news was out. Pictures were taken, including the AP photo of Lt. Silvashko and me which appeared on the front pages of newspapers around the world. The Press then left to file their stories and return for the next day's meetings.

By then, it was past midnight. The date was April 26. Our patrol was very tired, having gotten little sleep the night before. The Russians had to get back to their lines. We had made arrangements for our CO's to meet at ten o'clock that morning in Torgau. So back we went to Regiment to organize a fourteen-jeep patrol.

Since the four of us already knew the way to Torgau, our jeep led the convoy. This patrol, accompanied by Col. Adams, arrived in Torgau at dawn. The Press also arrived. It was on the 26th that most of the pictures of the link-up were taken, including the movie footage.

On the 26th, we learned that Lt. Albert Kotzebue's twenty-eight man jeep patrol from our 273rd Regiment had actually been the first to meet the Russians. Buck Kotzebue's patrol had also met part of the Fifty-eighth "Garde" Division. They made contact the previous day at Strehla, located on the Elbe about sixteen miles south of Torgau. Kotzebue had met the Russians at 12:30 P.M. - three and a half hours before we did. The Kotzebue Patrol therefore deserves credit for being the *first* American unit to link up with the Russians.

When the Robertson Patrol returned with the Russian delegation to the U.S. lines on the evening of April 25, we had met the Press without much delay. The news was flashed to the world. We got most of the publicity, as well as the credit for the first "official" link-up in Torgau. In the meantime, however, Buck and his men remained in the Russian lines overnight. He was not able to make contact with Division, let alone the Press, until after the "official" meetings at Torgau.

EVENTS . . . EFFECTS . . . AND THOUGHTS ON CHANGES . . .

by Lt. William D. Robertson, 1945
273rd Regiment, 1st Battalion S-2, Intelligence Officer
69th Infantry Division

(*Editorial note:* The title of this article has been edited for space considerations. The original title was *The Events Of April 25, 1945, And Their Effects On My Life, And My Thoughts On Changes Behind The "Iron Curtain" In The Past 50 Years*)

The events of Torgau certainly had an impact on my life. The members of our patrol were instant celebrities. We were issued clean clothes and flown to Paris for a little R&R, then to Rheims to present our home-made flag to General Eisenhower. We were all promoted, returned to Leipzig and received U.S. and Soviet decorations. I was flown back to the U.S. to become a speaker to participate in the 4th War Bond Drive in New York, Washington, and then to the West Coast to speak at various Aircraft Plants, Shipbuilding Yards, and Motion Picture Studios. All that was pretty "heady" stuff for a 21 year old.

Torgau, however, did not have any impact on my future career. My goal was always to return to College, and then I decided to go to Medical School.

I was discharged from the Army in 1946, and returned to UCLA, as a pre-med student. In 1947, I went to the University of California Medical School at Berkeley, San Francisco, California. I married a UCLA student in 1948. Her name was Nancy Quanstrom. She became a teacher.

I graduated from Medical School in 1951, rejoined the Army as an MD Intern in San Francisco, and was sent to the Army Hospital at Ft. Carson, Colorado. Our first child, Douglas, was born there. I left the Army again in 1953, and we moved to London, England, where I took a year of training in Neurology at Queen-Square Hospital. We next went to Oxford, where I started my Neurosurgical training. We moved back to Los Angeles in 1955, and I did General Practice for 2 years. Then I continued my Neurosurgical Residency training at UCLA. I completed training in 1961, entered private practice in West Los Angeles, and was appointed an Associate Clinical Professor in Neurosurgery at UCLA.

Our family grew up in Culver City in Los Angeles. We had four sons: Douglas, Richard, Donald, and Bruce. We lost a son, Donald, in 1979, and we lost Nancy to cancer in 1981. I retired from practice in 1984. My hobbies have included sailing, archaeology, and genealogy.

The events of April 25th, 1945, at Torgau, has added spice and interest at times through my life. Periodically, usually on Anniversaries of the event, there would be some newspaper interviews, etc. I first returned to Torgau on a 69th Division Tour in 1965 with my wife and one son. I went to Moscow on a U.S. State Department trip with my wife in 1975. Since 1985, it seems I've been to Torgau or Moscow almost every year. Sometimes these interesting trips have been sponsored by TV studios—York TV in Britain, Thames TV in Britain, and ABC in the U.S., doing documentaries.

I'm often asked if my experiences in 1945 and since have affected my attitude and feeling about Russia and her satellite nations throughout the "Cold War". I believe the honest answer to that is "No". My attitude has generally reflected that of our nation. It was Soviet intransigence and hostility and desire to export their form of government that brought on and perpetuated the Cold War. Only since the collapse of Soviet Communism and it's economy in 1985, have I become more optimistic. With the onset of "Glasnost" in '85-'86 came a sudden increase of frankness and freedom and open discussion. Then, almost unbelievably, came the fall of the Berlin Wall, re-independence of the satellite nations, and the re-unification of Germany. No one could have predicted all of this.

My impressions of Torgau and the GDR at various times: My wife and I first visited Torgau after the war in 1965, on a 69th Division Tour. We had a very limited tour of Torgau, and stayed in Leipzig. It was a "through the window" kind of tour, by bus, and we had almost no opportunity to spend time, meet the people, etc. It was a very ancient town, but seemed very drab and spiritless. So also was most of the GDR! Bullet holes unpatched, no paint on homes, few cars, no smiles on faces, coal piled on sidewalks, etc.

In 1985, Torgau and the GDR were much the same - drab and grey, and unchanged. East Berlin seemed to be re-building and appeared to be somewhat more prosperous. But the countryside seemed unchanged. Again we had no real chance to visit with people. Since 1985, I've been back to Torgau almost yearly. Only after Gorbachov came to power, followed by the fall of the Berlin Wall, have things seemed to change (to an outsider). In the past 4 years, I have seen many significant changes. Homes are being painted, repaired. New building is seen. Many more, and mod-

Photo of Robertson, Silvashko, and General Orlov taken in Torgau, Germany, April 1990. A copy of Yanks Meet Reds *is open to a picture taken of Orlov in 1945. (Photo by D. E. Philpott)*

ern, cars about, better roads, smiling faces, etc. My problem has always been my inability to communicate in German, so my impressions are from my "eyes" only.

Lt. William D. Robertson was born on January 7, 1924, in Los Angeles, CA. to Samuel N. Robertson and Laura Maude Cooper who had moved from Wisconsin. His father was from Scottish descent and his mother from German-British stock. Bill was 17 and in his last year of High School when the attack on Pearl Harbor occurred. He entered UCLA in the spring of 1942, and soon after joined the Enlisted Reserve Corp of the U.S. Army. He was called to active duty as a Private in the spring of 1943. While in basic training in Camp Roberts, California, he took and passed the OCS (Officer Candidate School) examinations. He was sent to UCLA with the ASTP group until openings occurred at Fort Benning, Georgia (the Infantry Officer Training School). He finished OCS in 1944, and was sent to the 69th Infantry Division in Camp Shelby, Mississippi, which was training for battle in the Pacific. He was assigned to 1st Battallion S-2, Intelligence Officer, 273 Regiment. In November 1944, the Division was ordered abroad, and went to Camp Kilmer, New Jersey, and then to England. The Division trained in the SE of England near Winchester. Many from our trained division were taken as replacements during the Battle of the Bulge. After new replacements arrived, the Division was sent to France in January, 1945, at the close of the Battle of the Bulge, and entered combat at the Seigfried Line at the Belgium Border. The Division was made part of General Hodges' 1st Army and fought through Germany to Leipzig, which was the largest city taken by the 69th Division. Then they made their way to the Mulde River. Next came the 4 man patrol that helped make history at Torgau, and the patrol became celebrities.

Dr. William D. Robertson, M.D.,
Retired since 1984

MY LIBERATION

by George Peck
Naval Ensign

(This story was previously published in Yanks Meet Reds *edited by Mark Scott and Semyon Krasilshchik, 1988.)*

On the afternoon of April 25, 1945, Sgt. Victor Berruti and I were sitting by the side of a road near Torgau, not far from Fort Zinna. Looking down the road, we caught a glimpse of a lone jeep disappearing around a bend.

"Looks like they're going away, Lieutenant," Victor remarked.

"Maybe they'll come back," I replied. "Let's sit here and wait for them."

Victor and I were liberated on that April day. On October 13, 1944, five of us Americans from the OSS had been captured near Turin, Italy, after a day long shoot-out high in the Alps. My German captors had found it hard to understand what I, a naval ensign, was doing at an altitude of nine thousand feet. But when they found out that we were in the intelligence service, they got the picture.

Our group was shipped off to Germany - well out of reach of the Italian partisans who had tried to free us. On November 9, I escaped from jail in the Bavarian town of Moosburg, only to be recaptured four days later. This escapade did little to endear me to my captors. It led to my being confined to solitary for almost five months - a lesson in patience. On about April 1, my companions and I were transferred to Fort Zinna. At that time, it was the only large military prison still operating in Nazi Germany. There, we were to stand trial as spies.

When we arrived at Fort Zinna, the Germans took us to a sort of outer office, where we were processed. A trusty of doubtful appearance stealthily approached us. He pointed to a stack of folders lying on a counter top. Each was marked with a large "T". Those he said, were our dossiers, and added:

"T" meint Tod!" ("D" means death!)

Fear fell upon us.

I was again separated from my companions. That evening, at nightfall, I could hear sounds coming from across the fields, sounds resembling small sticks being snapped in half. I heard them again, then realized that the firing squad was at work - a nightly event at Fort Zinna. Meditating in the gathering gloom, I realized that if God had meant me not to continue on earth, that would be all right too. A great sense of peacefulness came over me as I thought, "Thou preservist him in perfect peace whose mind is stayed on Thee."

About an hour later, I had a visitor. André Levacher, a French captain, seemed an angel of mercy. He said he knew all about our case. André told me not to worry, predicting that the Nazi military judges would not press the charges of espionage against us when they themselves were likely to be in the dock in the near future. And so indeed it turned out.

As he left my cell, André asked if I would like to be transferred to his cell, which he shared with Bertelsen, the Danish ex-Consul General. Would I! The next day, I moved in with them; we talked non-stop for twelve hours. André lived in Châlon-sur-Marne, and had seen his home destroyed twice - in 1914 and 1940. His crime was that after having been captured with the whole army on the Maginot Line, he had operated an underground railroad for escaped French POWs. Bertelsen was reticent about his own connections with the British underground as his case was still pending. His contributions to the conversation consisted of witty good humor and the passing on of many goodies sent down from Berlin by the Danish Foreign Office. He gave me four hundred cigarettes with which I bought an excellent Swiss-made German army watch.

One prominent German prisoner who frequently visited our cell was Gen. Oskar Ritter von Niedermayer, a scion of the Bavarian nobility and former chief of the *Wehrpolitisches Institut* in Berlin. As the American and Russian armies were advancing toward us from opposite directions, the General gladly shared his expert knowledge of military strategy with André, who in some ways was becoming the unofficial head of the prison.

"Like von Niedermayer, most of the two thousand or so prisoners in Fort Zinna were Germans who had fallen under the condemnation of the Nazis. By early April, all of us realized that the net was quickly closing in on the Third Reich. Reading the morning bulletins in the *Volkischer Beobachter*, we knew on about April 20 that the Russians were stalled two miles east of us across the Elbe, and the Americans twenty or so miles to the west on the banks of the Mulde."

When the front drew near, a field hospital moved in, filling the cellars of the fort with wounded soldiers. On April 23, orders came through to evacuate the fort. All were to withdraw with the remaining German forces to Bavaria, where the Nazis were to make a last stand in the so-called *Festung Europa*. The next day, André told the prison authorities that they could do what they pleased with the German prisoners, but that the Allied POW's and wounded would not leave. To my surprise, the authorities agreed. The German prisoners departed on the evening of the 24th, leaving the fort in the hands of the French, British, Russians, Italians, and us.

April 25, the great day, dawned in a cold drizzle. Up betimes to test our new freedom, we gathered in the front courtyard of the prison. There we witnessed a heart-rending scene which might have come straight out of the Thirty Years War - that other great German tragedy.

The Nazis were evacuating the field hospital. Ambulatory patients were hobbling along, some scantily clad and wrapped in blankets, others practically barefooted. The more seriously wounded were riding in commandeered farm wagons, the kind usually used to cart potatoes or manure. The wounded lying in the wagons were mercilessly joggled as the horses pulled the carts over the cobblestones.

Several of us approached the Nazi medical officer-in-charge and asked him to leave the badly-wounded Germans behind as an act of mercy. Of course, his job was to repair the broken bodies so that they could again serve as *Kannonenfutter*, but that was not his answer. He turned violently on us and launched into an invective which ended with the prediction, "In two months, we will push you Americans back into the North Sea!"

We thought he was crazy. Finally, the last cart passed through the gate of the ancient fortress. On its tailgate sat a Red Cross nurse with her feet dangling over the board. I saw tears streaming down her plain, German face.

André was in charge of the fort now. One of the first things he did was post a guard at the wine cellar of the fortress. He maintained that the wine, most of which was French, was by right ours. However, he didn't act fast enough to frustrate a very large and very wild Irishman in the British service, who got a skinful by 8:00 A.M. Paddy started breaking up the furniture and making a great row. We didn't know what to do until our staunch American sergeant, Victor Berruti, showed up. Victor never let us down in a pinch. He wheeled Paddy toward the entrance of Cell Block D, threw open the gate, and offered him any room in the house. Soothed by his amiable ruse, Paddy progressed into the lachrymose stage and submitted to being led to a bunk to sleep it off.

Like Paddy, each of us explored the joys of freedom in his own way. In addition to running the fortress, André led the French contingent in the preparation of a glorious celebration feast. The Russian lieutenant - the pilot Titov - had worked in the poultry yard up until our liberation; he contributed dozens of eggs and a supply of young spring chickens. The English captain, Lewis Lee Graham, had miraculously survived years of severe malnutrition, pneumonia, and the bombing of his prison; he wanted a good, long, hot bath - and got it. The Italian colonel reasserted his tarnished authority by having his enlisted men black his boots.

As for me, I was seized by a fear of anarchy. Because the Germans had left a vacuum in authority, I felt called upon to fill it. I asked André if I could see to the comfort of the Allied wounded. Readily agreeing, he lent me a smartly-cut French jacket to replace my worn GI overcoat. I now looked more like an officer. Victor found a silver bar to pin on my overseas cap. The illusion was effective, if perhaps confusing. The wounded – forty of so Russians and a handful of Americans – were carefully brought up from the cellar and installed in clean beds in an airy barracks.

Shortly after noon, someone rushed into the fortress with the electrifying news, "The Americans are here!" But it was a false report. Victor and I became impatient, and so went out at about three o'clock to look for the Americans. A warm sun had come out by the time we sat down by the road. The chestnut trees were just coming into bloom and we were glad to be out on our own.

We sat down on the side of the road. It was long, straight, and flat. It led across the plain to the west and - we hoped - to the Americans. We waited.

At 3:15 P.M., we spotted a tiny vehicle at the point where the road centered its lines of perspective on the horizon. As the spot grew larger, we saw that it was a jeep. The back seat was full of small arms. On the pile perched a GI corporal.

"Hiya, fellas!" he called out. Never have the accents of my native New York sounded sweeter. Like Victor, he was from the East Bronx. The two were soon in deep conversation about home addresses, delicatessens, and restaurants - food was an obsession with both POWs and GIs.

The commander of the patrol was Second Lt. William Robertson, who introduced himself as "Bill." He was from Los Angeles, and right now had more serious concerns on his mind.

"Are there any Germans in Torgau?" he asked.

"No," I answered, eager to be of service. "They pulled out this morning at about seven. But there may be a few *Volksturm* around." The *Volksturm* was that pitiable militia of old men and boys who were supposed to defend their homes.

"Where are the Russians?" Bill asked.

"At Brückenkopf, just across the river," we answered. "They came about two days ago and have stayed there."

"Let's see if we can find them!" Bill said.

Robertson admitted that he was not supposed to be there at all. His patrol had run ahead of the American lines, enticed by the great number of Germans who were anxious to give up their arms to the Americans instead of to the dreaded Russians. Hence, the pile of pistols, machine pistols, and tommy guns on the back seat of the jeep.

Bill gave us our pick of weapons, and invited us to join the patrol. The six of us drove on into Torgau itself. Bill then got out of the jeep and led four of us in echelon formation on each side of the street; Victor followed in the jeep. Here and there, a house was quietly on fire. No one took notice.

We came out onto the marketplace. Bill had a large white sheet which he planned to use as a flag whenever we got to the Russians. Victor and I said that this was not such a good idea as the Germans had been overdoing that tactic recently and the Russians would certainly take us for Germans. Someone said, "Let's paint it so it will look like an American flag."

This said, Bill went up to a hardware store, shot out the lock and pane of glass with his machine gun, and reached through to undo the latch. We found dry water paint, mixed up the colors, made three broad red stripes across the sheet, and painted a blue field in one corner. The spots where the blue paint didn't stick were meant to be stars. It was quite a flag; I had taken the precaution of tearing a corner from it to show doubting persons as proof that this whole experience was not a dream. Later, we heard, Bill gave it to Gen. Eisenhower, who is said to have passed it on to the Smithsonian – the nation's attic.

Coming out of the store, we found our way to Hartenfels Castle, right across the river from the Russian lines. The castle was a fortress built by Frederick the Great of Prussia in the 1740s after his victory over Saxony and Austria. It had a watchtower with a platform surmounted by a crown-shaped dome.

Having driven through the courtyard entrance to the castle, we raced up the stairs and came out high above the river, swirling below. The bridge had been blown up; the roadway was totally destroyed with only the twisted girders of the superstructure remaining. On the far side of the Elbe - about five hundred yards away - were the Russian lines. They had erected a series of earthworks running in front of the small military prison of Brückenkopf. A Russian armored truck stood in the lee of one of the few houses. Lying between the Russians and us were a wide, green field, the river with two web-like bridges spanning it, and the Torgau embankment.

We could see figures walking around behind the earthworks.

Briefly surveying the situation, Bill clambered up a rickety ladder in the belfry through a trap door to the open space under the dome. He climbed up over the platform onto the dome - more than a hundred feet above the Elbe - and began precariously waving the flag at the Russians.

No response.

I called up, "*Shout Amerikanskii soldatui!*" I had dreamed many times in the prison of being liberated by the Russians, and had got hold of a German Russian Soldier's Dictionary. I had learned all the expressions in the front of the book, especially words such as *drug* ("friend"), *daitye mnye khlyeb* ("give me bread"), *gyde...?* (where is...?"), etc.

Robertson was getting results. We could see heads peep out from behind the earthworks.

Then a red flare went up.

"Damn it!" Bill shouted, "I forgot the flare." (American patrols were supposed to carry answering green flares in case they met the Russians.)

From our side of the Elbe, scattered *Volksturm* fired a few sniper shots. This was enough for the Russians. They opened fire.

It was very impressive. The entire line blossomed with flashes of flame. From where we were, it looked like striking flints. The sparks mushroomed out; I could look down the middle to see the bullet coming.

We all ducked. But not Bill. He kept waving the flag. After a while, he got tired, and came down to the platform.

"Look," I told him, "I've got a friend at the fort, a Lt. Titov, who's a Russian pilot shot down over Stalingrad. He can talk to them in Russian."

Bill yelled down to Victor - still in the jeep - to high-tail it back to Fort Zinna and bring back the Russian lieutenant. After an interminable wait, the jeep reappeared, and Titov came puffing up the stairs. I began explaining the situation to him in German, which he did not understand very well. But Victor must have gotten the message across to him for the pilot sprang into the belfry and began yelling at the top of his large lungs in Russian, drawing out his syllables in long, mournful cries. I thanked our lucky stars that he was a husky fellow - in civilian life a hunter from Vladivostok - because he must have had to bellow for five minutes.

A few heads reappeared on the east bank. Soldiers began coming out from behind trees, out of shallow trenches. Titov must have been asking them to come down to the river. A few jumped over the earthworks.

Bill shouted, "Let's go!" and we all scrambled down the stairs, jumped into the jeep, and sped up onto the embankment.

The opposite fields were filling up with soldiers. We waved frantically and started running for the bridge. I asked Bill if I might come along with him, since I knew German and they might not have someone who knew English.

But Bill was already crawling on the twisted girders of the bridge. I followed close behind. A Russian sergeant had already got a good start toward us from the other bank. He met Bill and then I edged by. The girder was not wide. It was not easy to manage without falling into the rushing river below. But we made our way to the east bank where we were greeted by a group of Russians. All of us were jabbering, shaking hands, and slapping each other on the backs.

We asked the Russians where they had come from and they answered, "Stalingrad." Theirs was a unit of the Ukrainian army; they looked as though they had walked the whole way. There were almost no vehicles anywhere, except one truck and a few liberated horse wagons - so different from our own highly-mechanized forces. I was also surprised by their uniforms. Although ours were not exactly colorful, theirs seemed drab. They all wore frayed outfits, all but the commanding officer - a smartly uniformed major. A tall blond, he looked like Alexander Nevsky - the real one, not the actor who played the part in the Eisenstein film.

Bill and the Major sat down to exchange credentials and talk. I offered to serve as interpreter since the *lingua franca* in this part of Europe was not English - as it is now - but German. The Major fixed a hard stare on me and barked, "*Nyet!*" I had forgotten the Russian attitude which was that any POW was considered a treacherous deserter until proven otherwise.

As the two talked, I noticed another important difference between our armies - there were a number of women here dressed just like the men. They were paramedics. I had once known a Russian paramedic just like them who had been taken prisoner by the Germans. The job of these women was to administer first aid, no matter how hazardous the fighting. Many were killed in battle. I found out later that the proportion of battle-wounded who were saved was higher in the Russian army than in any other, including our own.

By this time, the celebration had gotten under way. One Russian soldier was firing a German bazooka into the river; the missile made a big splash and satisfying bang. The Russians passed around German schnapps as well as German cheese, sausage, bread, and chocolate. In the absence of much verbal communication, there was a lot of hugging and backslapping.

A Russian captain befriended me. His chest was covered with well-worn medals - not just the ribbons, but the whole medals. This heroic figure gave me a big hug, but it developed that he was not especially attracted to me, but to my 400-cigarette watch. The historic occasion, he said, should be memorialized by our exchanging watches and he offered me a woman's brass watch that was no longer working. He said my wife would like it. I was so astonished that I reluctantly agreed and was left with the thought that this shrewd fellow enjoyed historic occasions to his own advantage.

Sitting there in the light of the westering sun, I had time for reflection. This was indeed an historic occasion. For another person, I suppose, this mood would have seemed incongruous amid all the rejoicing. But I was an historian, one who had been deeply involved in political intelligence for several years. That afternoon, sitting on the banks of the Elbe, I remembered that the Spanish Civil War in which other "premature anti-fascists" like me had fought, had started nearly ten years earlier. The long struggle against the fascist dictatorships was finally coming to a close. Britain was saved. So too were France and Italy, though starved and battered. Jewish survivors of the death camps were being freed.

I was suddenly flooded with a warm surge of hope. That same day, the United Nations was being formed in San Francisco. The peace of the world was to be founded upon the friendship of our two great nations - the United States and Soviet Union.

Bill and the Major concluded their business; they arranged a meeting between their commanding officers, a meeting which took place the next day on a bridge farther down the river. "I've got to get back to the Mulde before sundown," Bill suddenly said. "It's nearly five. Let's get going!"

A Russian soldier discovered an abandoned motor launch by the river and jumped in. But because the motor wouldn't start, another soldier found a rowboat to ferry us across. On the west bank, we were joined by a Russian medical contingent, which followed us to Fort Zinna. They immediately evacuated the Russian wounded, leaving the Americans with us. Bill left Victor and me there, saying he would report our whereabouts. Help would arrive by morning, which it did.

The Russians didn't leave us right away. One of them came up to André and pointed to a seventeen-year-old German boy wearing an SS uniform. The Russian indicated by sign language that he wanted to shoot him. André well knew of the horrors of National Socialism. He knew the barbarous acts committed by the SS not only in the Soviet Union, but also in his own country. Yet he refused to surrender the young German. Instead, he sent the boy home - to his mother.

The sun was now setting. The feast prepared by the French residents of Fort Zinna was laid out on long trestle tables. We all sat down higgledy-piggledy, officers and enlisted men, French, British, Italian, and American. Our conversation was in French, which most of the men understood and some spoke. We drank our victory toasts in the wine of André's home region, Champagne. Our cooks and waiters had worked several seasons at Trouville, St. Malô, and the like. And so our celebration feast was a gourmet's delight - broiled spring chicken, fresh asparagus and new potatoes, all washed down with vintage Barsac. Dessert was apples - the first fresh fruit many of us had had for months - cheese, black bread, and more champagne.

But before joining that memorable celebration, I lay down on my bunk to rest. It was the first time I had really rested since morning, when I undertook the task of fighting my own fear of anarchy by burying the dead, comforting the sick, pacifying the drunks, and keeping the pillaging within bounds. The day had finally hit me. I began shaking violently, uncontrollably. My nervous system, which had lain quiet for so long, had endured too much.

André came over to say something. He looked intently at me, turned, and silently walked away. André was a civilized man.

POSTSCRIPT

The above written ten years ago seems to me to require no changes except the elimination of typographical errors. Since then, a new editor has asked for something different — reflections on what this experience has meant to me in the fifty years since that time. Certain discoveries or lessons seem to me to have emerged and become a part of what after all is most of my life.

First, it was in that prison cell listening to the stutter of the firing squad that I faced the inevitability of my mortality. Like most young people and specifically Americans, I had heard almost nothing about death and sort of assumed I would go on forever. Death was not a proper subject for conversation or even of the sermons I heard. The bell was tolling for someone else. It was an important discovery to realize that my life on earth was but a tiny part of the life force that was everywhere and eternal. Whatever happened to my body could not touch my relationship to God. I would go on to express this harmony and might even, for all I knew, get another go at it if this body were destroyed.

Second, I waited five months and ten days in prison mostly alone, long enough to get used to waiting. On the day after the events at Torgau, I "liberated" an Opel and drove west with a carload of allied POW officers to Leipzig. We drew up in a central square and I jumped out to find out at the American headquarters where to go next, apologizing to my friends for having to keep them waiting. They were quietly gawking at the crowds of real ordinary people. Our Parisian friend, Jacques Adler, said, "I don't think I'll ever again have trouble waiting." And so it has been for me too. We learned the patience that years of frustrated hopes and plans had taught Don Quixote. "They also serve who only stand and waite." (Milton)

Third, I learned that deprivation was no fun. Coming from a comfortable background, I sometimes envied those who could boast of rising out of limitation and need. No more. I now had my share: months of always being cold, not always but just about 22 hours a day because for brief periods after meals one was temporarily warm. Months of always being hungry, 22 hours a day. Later, I figured out that our prison fare of *Gemuese Eintopf* (vegetable soup) and bread gave us about 1100 calories a day and almost no fats, proteins, and vitamins, plus additions every two weeks from Red Cross packages if they arrived. No wonder that celebration dinner at Fort Zinna made such a deep impression. Celebrations still do and every day I thank God for a good appetite and try to spread the bounty.

> *Some hae meat and canna eat,*
> *And some wad eat that want it;*
> *But we hae meat and we can eat,*
> *And sae the Lord be thankit.*
>
> The Selkirk Grace

Fourth, slowly - oh so slowly - I learned to forgive. Before the war, I heard Hitler speak in the newsreels and my schoolboy German was good enough for me to understand him and shutter. Then I went to work for a famous German Jewish scholar, Theodore Adorno. My job was to render his German philosophical English into a semblance of American English, and so I learned in painful detail about the Holocaust then in progress and the virulence of anti-Semitism all over the world. This was the main reason I entered wholeheartedly into what seemed to me a just war. When I ended up in disciplinary confinement at Stalag VII A, one of our jailers was a sadistic sycophant and the other, a saint - perhaps a fair proportion in any army.

Anyway I had a lot to forgive, and it was a slow job. I found I did not want to share in what seemed the element of revenge at the Nuremburg trials. The attractions of hatred and punishment began to wane, not because they were unjustifiable but because they warped my life and didn't help them. Years later when our young son had a pal from Stuttgart, my wife and I decided to take him for a visit there. How would I find the Germans now? My first memorable experience was being stopped on the autobahn and verbally abused by an irate cop for what seemed to me a minor lapse. The officer seemed to me an interesting aberration to be experienced in any country and my efforts to calm him down were successful. The lack of irritation and fear felt good. Surely we must remember past horrors so that they be not repeated, but also we must truly forgive.

"Father, forgive them, for they know not what they do." Lu. 23:34.

Lastly the vision of peace in the world which I had that day on the banks of the Elbe has stayed with me ever since and steadily grown. As the Cold War was being cranked up by Churchhill, Truman, and Stalin, I never believed that America and Russia would go to war with each other, and so the whole brouhaha was irrelevant to me. It was not only the basic humanity of our peoples which stood against the calculations of politics but also the recognition that each of our countries was nearly completely self-sufficient in its own corner of the world. About twenty years after Torgau, I joined the Society of Friends (Quakers), but with the proviso that I could not accept its testimony against all wars. After all *my* war was a just war. Each Sunday I sat in silence enjoying the presence of God and learning to feel his power and her tenderness. *Slowly* the truth was borne in on me that it was better to be killed than to kill a fellow human. Jesus was right after all not to call up his legions but to suffer crucifixion. So for many Saturday mornings, I joined the silent vigils against the war in Vietnam, a war that today many Americans condemn. Then just a few years ago I joined the silent vigils against war in Irak, which not so many Americans condemn. God's truth does not change.

RECOLLECTIONS, MEMORIES, AND OBSERVATIONS

by Paul Staub
273rd Regiment, I. and R. Section, 1st Battalion, 69th Infantry Division

I can't believe it is almost 50 years since I first saw a Russian soldier on the bank of the Elbe River in Torgau, Germany. As I pause and look back on this momentous occasion I can recall the events of that day which led us to that historical meeting.

I was assigned to the Intelligence and Reconnaissance (I. and R.) Section 1st Battalion, 273 Regiment, 69th Infantry Division. My group had been assigned the task of organizing and directing the newly freed American and Allied P.W.'s, as well as hundreds of German soldiers who were ready to give up, to areas that were set up around the town of Wurzen. In addition, there were thousands of displaced persons whose carts and wagons lined the roads.

It was at this point that Lt. Robertson, Cpl. McDonnell, Pfc. Huff and myself were sent to evaluate the situation. Traveling North by jeep, we headed toward Falkenhain. Along the route we ran into several groups of German Soldiers who wanted to find the Americans. All were disarmed and sent back to Wurzen. I signed and gave safe passage passes to some of these groups (I later found out that some of these German soldiers showed up in Wurzen).

Near the town of Zachorna, we encountered the largest group of Germans—a Major with a company of men—who gladly surrendered and were also sent back to Wurzen.

As we continued on, we came across a large group of refugees — wagons — around Frauwalde. These too were sent to Wurzen. The trip proceeded with little or no resistance. The civilians seemed glad to see Americans and were very cooperative. We found a British Soldier who had been hidden by a German, quickly armed him, and directed him to the American lines. Then there was a skirmish with two S.S. men who we took as hostages and put on the hood of our jeep.

Following the main road which led to Sitzenroda, we met 30 freshly freed British P.W.'s. They reported that there were American wounded and P.W.'s in Torgau. As we started up, we ran into five more German Soldiers who wanted safe conduct passes. These were given to them and they were directed towards Wurzen.

I believe it was at this point that we started thinking Russian troops must be nearby. On the trip to Torgau, we stopped civilians and asked if they had seen any Russians. None had. We commandeered a white bed sheet, rolled it around a pole and put it in the back seat — just in case.

Continuing along, we came across a P.W. camp just outside of Torgau. This camp held men of all armies and all nations. We ordered the two S.S. men off the hood of the jeep and turned them over to the camp. After unloading the arms we had collected during our trip, we proceeded through the main part of Torgau. Hearing shooting, we speculated that the Russians would be there. Even though we carried the white flag with the hope that the Russians would not shoot, the small arms and rifle fire continued. We decided to turn the white flag into an American flag. After all, we weren't surrendering. We were hoping to meet an ally. We broke into a drugstore to get something to make red and blue colors. We quickly dabbed the chemicals and dyes onto the bed sheet, in an effort to make it look like an American flag. As we continued through Torgau, we entered the courtyard of a castle which was located about 300 yards from the Elbe River. Somehow we knew that the Russians were on the other side of the river.

Robertson and I climbed to the top of the tower, waved our homemade flag and tried to get the Russians to stop shooting and recognize that we were Americans and friends. They in turn fired up green flares which we later found out was the recognition signal. Someone suggested that we send back to the P.W. camp and get an individual who spoke Russian. This was done. The freed Russian P.W. was sent to the top of the tower where he yelled at the Russians on the East bank. Before you knew it, the Russians were coming across the bridge. Robertson and Huff headed for the East over the bridge and the meeting of the two Allies took place in the center.

McDonnell and I stayed with the jeep and equipment. Soon there were Russian Soldiers around us and I know they were as happy to see us as we were to see them. They showed us pictures of their families and we did the same. Although we did not speak the same language, we understood each other. It seemed to me a bottle of something appeared and we toasted each other several times.

Shortly afterwards, Robertson and Huff came back along with four Russian Soldiers and we left to go back to Wurzen. Thus the contact was made.

My feeling about the men that we met was and is that they are no different than we were. They were anxious to get the war over and get on with their lives, just as we were. They loved their country and their families just as we did. They liked a good joke and a good time. Who doesn't? I think this feeling of camaraderie still exists. Even during the Cold War, there were always groups of those who were at the Elbe River reaching out for each other.

On April 25, 1955, which was the 10th Anniversary, I was privileged to be with Vice President Nixon, Senators Douglas and Potter. We were broadcasting a message of hope and friendship over the Radio Liberation to those behind the Iron Curtain.

In 1975, the Russian Embassy in Washington again celebrated the Occasion. Frank Huff and I attended. The attention that we received was friendly and we were made to feel extremely welcome.

I have been approached several times over the past years by various Russian reporters, writers, and photographers as to my feelings then and now about the men I met at the Elbe River. My feelings have not changed over the years. They were just like us then, and we were like them.

It was a great moment for me and I would do it over again if I could.

One of Staub's famous pictures showing Robertson (kneeling) and Huff (holding the flag). (Photo provided by P. Staub)

"HOW <u>COULD</u> I FORGET?"

by William "Bill" R. Beswick
273rd Regiment, 661 Tank Destroyers
69th Infantry Division

April 25th, 1945, was one of the happiest days of my life, if not the happiest. The "FIGHTING 69TH" Infantry Division had met the Soviet Union's Armed Forces. We had cut Hitler's FASCISTS and NAZI Armies in half!

At that time, I do not remember meeting any of the German people of the Torgau area. I believe that everyone had left, expecting a lot of fighting. There was some, but not much, as I remember and I believe that I have a good memory.

After we had been in Torgau for five days, we were directed to move to the Kitzchen area to secure it. We were to meet up with some of the German citizens. We, as individuals, hired some of the women to wash our clothes. We gave them some small treats, such as fruit or cookies for their work. We had no money except invasion money and that was no good to them. We were treated and respected very well by the people of the villages. There was a small beer garden in Zitzen that some of us frequented. It had a pool type game and some of us whiled away our time playing this.

I was stationed in a small village near Zitzen. I was to write passes for the women to travel from one village to another to obtain food. I had a young high school girl as a secretary and translator. I was not given any funds to pay her, but when my meals came, I always obtained enough food for her as well as myself. After my job here was finished, I was moved to another village where there were three young German children; a brother aged twelve, his sister aged ten, and a friend of the brother aged twelve. I also obtained food for them each time my food was brought to me and gave them small treats, such as fruit or candy. They were very delightful children. I can't believe that they knew a war was fought in their area. I believe they were very sad when I left to come home.

I never had any more contact with any German people until November, 1983.

One quiet evening while reading my newspaper, I received a phone call from LeRoy Wolins whom I did not know. He was a close friend of Joe Polowsky and asked me if I knew Joe. I told him that I didn't, but had heard of him.

After talking to me awhile, he asked me if I would go to Joe's funeral as a friend of the family. It was to be held in Torgau, Germany. I had been invited to go to Europe on several occasions, but wasn't able to go. I told him that I would make this trip. He said my plane tickets would be at the Richmond, Virginia, airport. Sure enough, they were there. I still had a couple of days before I was to leave. I had to go to Washington, D.C. to obtain my papers and passports. I hadn't been to Torgau or Germany since 1945.

I left for Chicago two days later to meet the Polowsky family, a very nice family, indeed. In fact, I had Thanksgiving Dinner with them. We visited together for about three hours before LeRoy Wolins arrived. He was ready to leave for O'Hare airport in Chicago, Illinois. On arrival at the airport, we met Charles Forrester from Greer, South Carolina. Charles had known Joe Polowsky because they had been on the same patrol that met the Soviets on the Elbe River in Torgau, Germany, in 1945.

Charles and I were to attend the funeral on November 26, 1983, as friends of the family. On the bus from Luxembourg airport to Frankfurt, Joe's son, Ted, asked us what we thought about professional pallbearers. We both told him that we did not think it was personal enough, so Ted asked us if we would serve as pallbearers. We agreed to do so. On our arrival at the Torgau Cemetery, we met Russian General Alexei Gorlinski and Colonel Ivan Samchuk, friends of Joe. All had met on the bank of the Elbe River in 1945 and had kept in touch until Joe's death in 1983. They agreed to

Joe Polowsky's funeral in Torgau. (Photo by V. Klug)

serve as pallbearers. Two American Soldiers from the Berlin Garrison also served as pallbearers and folded the flag that was presented to Ted.

It began to rain steadily as we were half way to the grave site. I had left my raincoat on the bus and didn't have time to return for it. We put Joe's body over the grave and moved off to one side. The rain continued to pour. A German man standing next to me gradually put his umbrella over me so I wouldn't get any wetter. At the same time, he was getting soaked. This was the first time for me to meet an East German. I soon discovered that they were extremely nice people and very accommodating.

After the services were complete, we returned to the Central Hotel in Torgau and enjoyed a fine German-style dinner with some of the Germans. Among them was Vice Mayor (Bürgermeister) Wolfgang Gerstenberg, who is the present Mayor of Torgau. He is an extremely nice person. With the help of translators, we all sat around and talked for about three hours with some of the Garrison Soldiers from Berlin and civilian employees of the Garrison, several U.S. correspondents and the Soviet General and Colonel. Many Torgau citizens were present and participated in the discussions.

I was soaked to the bone and wanted to go to my room and change into my dry clothes. Soviet General Gorlinski said, "NOT YET!, NOT YET!", and the first thing I thought about was, "WHAT HAVE I GOTTEN MYSELF INTO NOW". I almost wished I'd stayed home. About half

William Beswick in 1945. (Photo provided by William Beswick)

an hour later, General Gorlinski said, "It looks like you are all wet. Let's go get you into some dry clothes". As we prepared to leave on the bus, the two Soviet officers boarded with us and their car followed with the General's two Aides.

One incident occurred that I thought amusing. General Gorlinski's Aides were two Soviet Officers who were at least six feet nine inches tall. I attempted to take their picture. They were quick to say, "No". That was OK. I understood because this was during the period when the Wall was still up. When they saw me go to the cemetery with General Gorlinski, they began wanting to pose for me so I would get a good picture. Wouldn't you know, the film didn't turn out. So, I really DIDN'T get their picture after all.

LeRoy Wolins' ability to speak fluent Russian took care of any problems.

We learned on arriving in Leipzig that the Soviet officers had had a very appetizing banquet prepared for us at the Merkur Hotel and they did not want us to arrive too early. We enjoyed it thoroughly. After the meal and some more visiting, we prepared to leave the hotel for the train station for our trip back to Frankfurt. The whole crowd accompanied us to the railroad station that we had fired at way back in 1945. You could not see any shell marks on the structure. It had been well repaired.

I must state here that the German people combined all their talents and efforts to clean and repair their country into excellent condition. This is what I learned when I journeyed to their country in 1985.

I was also fortunate to attend the Memorial Services in 1987 for Lt. Albert "BUCK" Kotsebue at the Arlington, Virginia, Cemetery; the sight of the "UNKNOWN SOLDIER'S" Tomb. At these very impressive services, I had the pleasure of meeting Buck's daughter, Deborah, a very dignified young lady.

All of these happenings, plus the fact that I traveled through the same German towns and villages where we had engaged in combat in 1945, encouraged me to find out if any of the other members of the 69th Infantry Division might be interested in

Joe Polowsky's gravesite in Torgau. (Photo by D. A. Philpott)

returning to Germany for our Fortieth Anniversary of "EAST MEETS WEST". I was tremendously surprised when I received responses from over two hundred people interested in a tour like this. One hundred and fourteen people finally went. All enjoyed every minute of the journey, especially visiting with the German children and adults. It was unforgettable.

While visiting in the Soviet Union in 1989, I was asked if there was any difference between the So-

German children befriended by William Beswick. (Photo provided by William Beswick)

viet and the American people. My reply was basically that we are all the same even though our languages and customs are different. I feel this way about the Germans too.

I want to make one point clear here. Most, if not all of us went to war against Hitler, his fascism and Nazism — not against the German people. They are very much like Americans.

I learned many years ago about oppression and the people of the world. There has been lots of it. I made up my mind that I would do all that I possibly could to prevent it. In a speech I made in Torgau, Germany, April 25th, 1990, I told how I felt about the oppression of the people.

We traveled to Germany in 1990 with about the same number of people that the 1985 tour had. The members are still talking about the excellent manner in which we were treated.

I cannot forget the number of Soviet Veterans that joined us in Torgau. I went through various channels and was told the next week that we would have about seventy-five join us; almost the same number of Soviet Veterans as American Veterans. Many new friendships were made as well as some old ones renewed. This is as it should be. We had a matching number of Soviets join us each trip.

I hope that our forthcoming journey for our "FIFTIETH ANNIVERSARY" in April, 1995, will be equally as memorable. I've met many Germans and I hope that I've established good relationships with them as I always enjoy visiting this very interesting country and its people. I'm looking forward to it again.

On my visit to the former East Germany in April, 1985, I had lunch with several Bürgermeisters and other officials of some of the towns and cities. We had a conversation about the "FRONTIER" as it was called, or the "FENCE BOUNDARY" between East and West Germany. After asking them several questions, I asked each of them if they would like to see the "FRONTIER" removed. After a long silence and discussion among themselves, they all replied, "YES". Then they asked what I thought. I replied that it might be great to see it all become one country again. One of the Bürgermeisters (Mayors) asked me how long I thought the "FRONTIER" would remain in place. I don't know if they thought I had some inside information or what. I responded that I thought it would be removed within "FOUR OR FIVE YEARS". This conversation took place April 22, 1985.

Sure enough, the Frontier was abolished on November 9, 1989 - four years and seven months later. Imagine my surprise when my son Alan came home from work and told me that the WALL had been removed. I'd been working in the yard most of the day and didn't know history was being made. Can you visualize my amazement when I heard my prediction had come true? I don't know if the man would appreciate me giving his name here, but immediately after the demise of the Frontier, he responded to my letter that I had written to him and the others for the very gracious way that they had welcomed us. He wrote the response in December, 1989. I had written him in May, 1985. He asked me if I remembered our conversation about the demise of the wall. I have only one comment. "HOW <u>COULD</u> I FORGET?"

I have enjoyed my visits to the various countries of the world. I have learned some of their customs and how to recognize and appreciate them.

All of this has made me a more tolerant person, especially of the oppressed people. Everyone should feel as I feel.   *Bill Beswick, July 31, 1994*

JOE POLOWSKY

by Irene Polowsky Rounds

Joe Polowsky was born in Chicago in 1916, as the third child of Jewish Russian immigrants. My grandparents fled Czarist Russia just after the turn of the century. Like many immigrants, they came to America for freedom from persecution and a better life.

They settled in a Russian community in Chicago, opened a grocery business and worked long, hard hours during difficult economic times. The family loved America and all she stood for.

My father was a quiet, private man. He was very bright and had a curious and analytical mind. He enjoyed English literature and writing about the human condition. He had a tremendous knowledge of history and a love of botany. He developed his scientific theories into a book he later named *Principia*; it is a work of biology with a philosophical component. He had hoped to have it in publishable form, but the war broke out. His life took on a different direction. Perhaps it was his destiny.

The war had a profound effect on him; it was the oath at the Elbe at the crux of it when the American and Russian soldiers linked up at the Elbe River, deep inside East Germany, which signified the end of the war. This was an event which remained with him for the rest of his life.

He was a spiritual man, allowing God to direct his life. He remembered the feeling of crossing the Elbe. It reminded him of when the Israelites crossed the Jordan River into the land of Canaan, the Promised Land. Just as God had delivered the Israelites long ago, he felt that the link-up between the Russians and the Americans was symbolic of God's deliverance. The soldiers swore an oath to work for friendship and peace, in the name of God, one another and to the millions who perished during the war.

After returning to the U.S., the world faded away from Joe's mind for a few years. As he returned to school to complete his studies, he could no longer ignore the world around him. On April 25th, 1947, he dropped out of school and pledged that he would do what he could to resurrect that oath. As a result, he attempted to make April 25th an international day of peace. Since the U.N. was also born on April 25th, 1945, he started there, petitioning the U.N. delegates from all over the world. The Philippines, Costa Rica and Lebanon had sponsored a resolution to this effect, but the Korean War broke out. Just like many times later, there was to be progress followed by obstacles.

Like Moses of the Old Testament, he seemed to wander in the desert for almost forty years.

His walk in the desert would have patches of oasis, which would restore his hope, but it would quickly fade in the form of disappointment, and he would wander further along. He knew God's work would not be easy, especially when dealing with the dark forces of this world, which he first addressed in a statement in 1951: "There can in this world be only a relative and never an absolute security, a world at peace, a strong U.N., a show of good faith on the part of the Soviet Union against any real threat, and give the Soviet Union a reasonable security. A Soviet occupation of the Milky Way and neighboring galaxies could not begin to satisfy the unreasonable and unattainable concepts of Soviet security, which come from the absence of peace of mind. And if the Soviet Union should push out into and occupy the outer reaches of an expanding universe, what if it should, to its dismay, there be confronted by the Almighty it has been running away from all the time."

The Soviet feeling of insecurity derives fundamentally and inevitably from its renunciation from God. If there is no trust, no faith in God, how can there be trust and faith in one's fellow man, without whom there can be no feeling of security? How can there, except under the fatherhood of God be a brotherhood of man.

As the above statement addresses the atheistic society the Soviet Union had become, my father became acutely aware of the Soviet spiritual oppression of its people. His concern plunged him into deeper sense of commitment. He had realized the magnitude of this serious problem. When one is not accountable to God, no telling what evil may surface. That was his dilemma. Only just a few years ago, millions of Jews were exterminated at the hands of evil, and the world asks how did this happen? Then came the evil of progression of the nuclear arms build-up.

As addressing the American position, he writes: "Men are born, men live and men die in a certain time under certain conditions with a given set of problems before them. Confronted with specific problems, one can avail oneself of opportunity or let it slip by. In an immediate, practical sense, our objective must be, by measuring up to our responsibilities, to leave Americans of the next generation in a tenable position. We, of this generation, may be sure that our babes in arms will be at least as wise as us, and in all probability much wiser. If we, in our generation, do what we can to secure the peace, if we leave them in a tenable position, they will assuredly further secure the peace for themselves and the next generation. If, as

Children of Torgau wearing "Hands Across the Atlantic" t-shirts. The young twins are sitting on the shoulders of 69th Inf. veterans Delbert Philpott and James Carroll. Irene Rounds helped form the "Hands Across the Atlantic" organization to increase understanding between nations by having German and American children correspond as pen-pals. (Photo by E. Bräunlich)

Joe Polowsky speaking to Torgau citizens in 1959. (Photo provided by the Torgau Kulturhaus)

much through errors of omission as errors of commission, we pass on to our young-sters an untenable moral, economic, and political position. Even if they have the wisdom of Solomon, the patience of Job, and the strength of Samson, we shall have delivered them on to their ruin. The initial moral advantage is ours. We cannot fail to have the moral courage to take the moral initiative and assert our moral leader-ship. We have had a noble past; we must assure our babes in arms as noble a fu-ture."

As a voice defending these moral principles, he passionately addressed nuclear arms issues. During the 1960's, especially in the latter part, he helped support the United Nations Nuclear Non-Proliferation Treaty, also known as the NPT. As the treaty was gaining momentum, the Russians invaded Czechoslovakia, once again diverting the eyes of the world from an important project. I remember him peti-tioning world and U.S. leaders, urging them to support the treaty. However, this was a very tumultuous time in the world.

As the masses protested the Vietnam War, he would stand a lone vigil every April 25th, on the Michigan Avenue bridge in downtown Chicago overlooking the Chicago River. He would tell people about the Elbe, handing out photocopies of the Stars & Stripes "Yanks Meet Reds." Other years, he would hold a sign, "Halt the spread of nuclear weapons. Save the NPT," with an accompanying flyer ex-plaining the importance of the treaty. Sometimes a sympathetic reporter would interview him and an article would appear in the newspaper. But mostly, people would pass by, accept a flyer and throw it in the nearest trash can. Sometimes he would invite me to go, but I always had an excuse not to. It was too painful to see the rejection and apathy of the crowds. But his strength and courage did not come from others. It came from a deep belief that God was orchestrating his efforts. As when we heed to the will of God, we have to have faith in the things we do not see.

His last efforts in support of the NPT were directed at Israel. In a statement, he writes, "That Israel would fulfill its historical, biblical and moral mission by ratifying the Nuclear NPT and the exemplary sacrifice by Israel of its nuclear weapons potential in the interest of world peace and security would excite the admiration, the congratulations of mankind, gain for Israel a great and honored place among the nations of the world."

His last trip abroad was to Israel in 1981 with hopes of gaining their support for the NPT. But, as many times before, his voice was not heard. Stranded without money to pay his hotel bill or trip home, the U.S. State Department paid his expenses and secured his passport until payment was made in full. But his heart was not discouraged as he expressed gratitude.

My retirement from the wars — at the conclusion — I can look at it with some perspective, now that it's over — of a 20th century epic of extraordinary accomplishment, the good fruits of which will become more and more manifest with the passage of time. It was an effort, in its duration of 36 years, its difficulty, its perseverance, its largeness of scope in a worthy cause, of Homeric, of biblical proportions, touching three generations, beginning with my swearing of the oath at the Elbe River, shortly before the end of WW-II in 1945, and the fulfillment of that oath, after memorable victories along the way, in 1981, during my recent trip to Europe and the Mideast. I stayed the course, and to those who helped along the way, my thanks indeed, since it was a real victory for the best in all of us, thanks to all.

Less than two years later, his health failed and he was diagnosed with a terminal form of cancer. He went public with an appeal to be buried at the Elbe.

In one of his last statements, he writes: "I often dream of the Elbe River, of that spring day, a generation ago, when the soldiers of the East and West met with high resolve, on the same day the U.N. was born a half a world away and in my dreams, the sea of dead men, women and children, the little girl with play crayons in one hand, the doll in the other, at the river's edge, are not dead, but asleep, awaken, and join in the rejoicing all about them, and swear with the rest of us never to forget that day when we met as friends to build a better world together. I want to go back to the Elbe."

The last days of Joe Polowsky's life were spent trying to collect funds for burial expenses. Also, to gain permission from the Communist authorities to be buried in Torgau, by the Elbe, in East Germany, which was then behind the Iron Curtain under Soviet rule.

He writes, "My view is that the ground at Torgau, my burial site, was paid for with the spilling of the blood of the soldiers of the World War II allies of the East and the West to rid Germany and the rest of the world of Hitlerism. While we Americans and Russians were meeting at the relatively peaceful field at Torgau's environs at noon on April 25th, 1945, with the smell of lilacs in the air, the troops of the massed Soviet forces 70 miles to the north were beginning to engage in the terribly bloody battle for Berlin. So my burial ground is paid for. My life has been a lifelong love affair with the stars and stripes. My coffin will be draped with the American flag, and I believe I have served the United States faithfully as well in war and in peace."

He died October 17th, 1983, in Chicago, without the funds nor the approval from the Communist authorities. However, he died knowing that somehow, some way God would see this happen.

Miraculously, ten thousand dollars needed for burial expenses was obtained from kind and caring people and the Communist authorities granted his wish. On November 26th, 1983, his body was brought to his final resting place, with an American flag covering his coffin, accompanied by two American military honor guards, two Russian generals and two American WW-II vets, who were also at the Elbe link-up.

In August 1989, the Berlin Wall came down, Communists no longer permeating the land, the people of Torgau are free to celebrate as they wish, and yearly, they have festivities for Elbe Day, which brings crowds from all over. Many people visit my dad's grave, with heartfelt thanks for his efforts over the years. It makes my heart rejoice to know that his life was not in vain, when I see today the good that has come. Yes, God is faithful to those who love him.

Irene Polowsky Rounds

It has been said that the U.S. and the U.S.S.R. can never at any time in the future become friends. Perhaps. But the lilacs bloom every spring in Central Europe, from the Baltic to the Mediterranean, as they did on April 25th, 1945, at Torgau. The mystic chords of memory of April 25th, 1945, in San Francisco (founding place of U.N.) and the Elbe River are not dead. 1983 is important, but what of 1984 and the years beyond? Something mutually satisfactory in some still unforeseen way will have to be worked out — and all the while Joe Polowsky being buried at Torgau on the Elbe River cannot but have a comforting, creative, positive effect upon events. Joe Polowsky (October 3, 1983)

THE BRIDGE AT TORGAU

by Eric Schultze,
former Lance Corporal,
57th Grenadier Battalion

I was wounded on January 4, 1945, while fighting in the Luxembourg area and this resulted in my being taken to a hospital in the Limburg/Lahn area. I was considered well enough to be released on March 16, 1945, and given a 15 day furlough for further recuperation. As soon as I was released, I traveled to my parent's home in Torgau at Backerstrasse 14. When the furlough ended on March 31, 1945, I reported to the Third Company Battallion - Southwest in Torgau. They transferred me to the Infantry and immediately assigned me to an anti-aircraft gun for the defense of Torgau.

The last available soldiers in the area were gathered up, resulting in the formation of three companies within the Battalion. The total force consisted of about 150 men, a force that would be equal to one infantry company in the American army.

About the 20th of April, the Pioneers were ordered to place explosives on the Torgau Bridge in the span areas that were directly over the Elbe River. The Pioneers' orders were to blow up the bridge in the event that a possible crossing by the Russians appeared imminent. One Torgau citizen approached the Pioneers and asked them not to blow up the bridge. The Pioneers replied that orders were orders and that unless rescinded, they would have to obey them and set off the explosives to destroy the bridge when the orders were handed to them.

The Russians approached Torgau from the east side of the river on April 24, and began their attack by firing Stalin Organ Rockets into the city. This rocket launcher consisted of six tubes arranged in parallel and capable of rapidly firing their rockets. This resulted in the death of two of our citizens and general confusion over what to do. Consequently, the Pioneers blew the bridge up at 3:30 AM on the 25th to prevent the Russians from crossing at that point.

The Americans were also rapidly advancing towards us. There was only a 30 kilometer corridor running northeast along the left side of the Elbe River which was still free of the approaching armies. It was obvious that the war was all but over and that further resistance was useless. Our defending force began to disband. I and a friend decided to walk northeast towards Worlitz. Others began to leave in other directions. This explains why Torgau wasn't defended on the afternoon of the 25th when the American patrol arrived.

We met a German patrol on the way to Worlitz and the officer immediately drew his pistol and demanded to know where we were going. I knew that he could shoot us if we didn't have orders for our travel, so I saluted and quickly answered, "Sir, I have orders to proceed to Worlitz."

The officer thought a minute and then slowly put his gun away. After what seemed a very long time he said, "All right, then you may proceed." My quick thinking no doubt saved our lives. I don't know if he believed me, considered the war over or was just worrying about his own survival.

I located civilian clothes upon arriving in Worlitz and exchanged them for my uniform. Later, when I obtained a bicycle, I rode to Torgau on the 27th. As I peddled into Torgau, I observed an American laying on his back with his rifle over to one side, his feet propped up on a rock and a music box blaring out loud music. I could hardly believe my eyes. This would never happen in the German Army. A German soldier would be in serious trouble if he ever let go of his gun and did not have it in front of him at all times. I had to laugh at this situation and thought that the Americans might be somewhat informal in our dealings with them.

I continued to live in Torgau and developed a successful business making and replacing window glass of all sizes.

*(**Ed. note:** "Pioneers" were Engineers.)*

THE FINAL WEEKS OF THE WAR

by Willi Hasemann
former German officer

(*Editor's Note*: The original title of the following article, *The Final Weeks of the War in 1945 in Torgau and the First Encounter with the U.S. Troops*, has been edited for space considerations.)

As the year 1945 started, all Germans hoped for a quick end to this war. Not only were the soldiers on the front tired of war, but after over 5 years, everyone in the homeland also wanted peace. I was then a Lieutenant of the Panzerabwehr with 20 other young officers. We were sent to Munster-Lager to be retrained as an anti-tank unit and were very glad to be in our homeland for several months.

After completing this course, we were given orders to go to Potsdam and Berlin during the first days of April. We were to go there to defend the area around the capital. Meanwhile, the troops of the Western Allies were on the Rhine River and the Russians were approaching the Oder.

We believed the immediate future would be bad because there would still be very hard fighting in Berlin. That was authenticated afterwards as many of my good friends from our trainee group lost their lives in the last days of the war. As for me, I was offered the opportunity not to travel immediately to Berlin, but to first spend a leave with my parents in the Bad Liebenwerda District. Here I met a school-friend who had been appointed an officer in Torgau only 30 km away. I learned from him that Torgau had been declared a fortress and I could come immediately as an officer for the anti-tank company. I joined him in the middle of April 1945, and became one of the major battle commanders.

Freiherr von Schlotheim was appointed as Company leader. Our headquarters were located in Hartenfels Castle and it became necessary to use the castle as a military field-hospital. The command group's orders were to defend Torgau from the East as well as from the West. The anti-tank company set up artillery pieces on streets leading into town and on the track-lines. The concentration of the defense was in the eastern direction. We spent some very quiet days in Torgau with very good food that we had received from the supply warehouse in Torgau. The American troops had penetrated Eilenburg and had paused on the Mulde River.

On April 20, 1945, the Russian troops reached Zwethau, Beilrode, and Graditz and finally remained at the bridge-head just across from Torgau. Surprisingly, there was no further aggression and no bigger skirmishes followed except small annoying fire from machine guns and grenade throwers. We did not find out at that time which objectives the American and Russian authorities were pursuing and why they didn't try to capture Torgau.

In the evening of April 23rd, all the officers were called together for combat instructions by the commanders. Everyone was nervous and asking themselves what was going on and whether it made sense to continue. We were happy to be told we would leave Torgau early the following morning, April 24th. The fighting group in Torgau had received orders from the commander to march immediately in the direction of Coswig and to cross over the Elbe and connect with Wenk's Army. Our anti-tank company listened. We were to start marching after all the cannons were exploded. When all the troops that had been east of the Elbe had crossed over the Elbe, both bridges were to be blown up. This was the command for the engineers. The Elbe bridges had been prepared for the blast for several days.

The officer of the engineers, a captain, had received a quite disagreeable and also very absurd command. He told me after the meeting that he was in a situation in which he preferred to prevent the destruction of the bridge, but it could cost him his life if he didn't execute the command. One simply hoped that the Russians would not attack our withdrawing formations. It was known to everyone, however, that the bridges could not be immediately constructed again and would be needed to supply the population with necessities after the war.

I did not have these misgivings because we just had some military equipment to destroy. They would not be required in any capacity after the end of the war to serve the population. So at dawn on April 24th, our cannons were exploded without having delivered one shot and the soldiers then gathered in the courtyard of Hartenfels Castle. One horse-drawn wagon with a coachmen stood ready for our military company as requested by our commander. The personal belongings of the soldiers were stowed and, in addition, we had received ample food. Then we ourselves followed the "route march" command to move in the direction of Bad Düben. The procession went through the mostly deserted city. After Weidenhain, a small village, we left the main road and walked across the Dübener Heide in the direction of Söllichau.

By the late afternoon, we found quarters in a barn near a forester's house and spent the night there. During the night, several soldiers and noncommissioned officers left us and hurried to the Americans in Bad Düben which was about 5 km away. You told yourself that they wanted to finish the war "in one piece". We recognized this war-tired feeling and the uncertain future along with the many older civilians that stood on the street and wanted us to tell them where the war would take us and when it would finally end.

On the morning of April 25th, we marched further in the direction of Coswig via Gräfenhainichen and Oranienbaum. At the outskirts of Oranienbaum, there was a surprise for us. Some 200 meters ahead, an American jeep with a mounted machine gun came around a curve from another street in the direction of Dessau.

Our soldiers jumped immediately to the side, looking around for cover from the trees and brought their guns into readiness. I remained standing on the street shouting loudly, "Don't shoot", to my men and waved at the slowly approaching jeep. Probably their personnel was equally as surprised as we were. After exchanging military salutes, I stood with a Lieutenant and 3 soldiers opposite me. When asked, "Do you speak English?", I answered, "Yes". We were quickly surrounded by German soldiers because everyone was curious and wanted to see American soldiers for the first time up close and were eager to see what would happen. The Americans seemed astonished at that moment because they were facing a "superior force". It was the first time they stood in the middle a group of German soldiers.

They also asked for directions. There was no feeling of mutual hostility and an informal atmosphere rapidly developed. This was my first chance to practice the English I had learned in school and I struggled to remember all the right words. An American offered me a cigarette, but I declined with thanks because I was a nonsmoker. Not being able to give me a cigarette, the American quickly reached into his pocket and, with a friendly smile, gave me a package of army chocolate. He

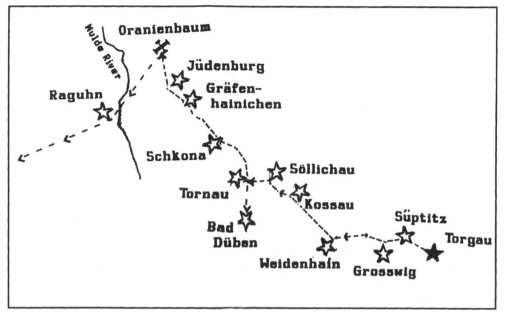

Route of W. Hasemann from Torgau to Raguhn. (Drawing of map by D. E. Philpott, D. A. Philpott and R. Studera based on W. Hasemann's information.)

explained to me that they were not looking for contacts with the Germans, but would like to push forward to the head of the Russian Army. It seemed strange to me that giving up to the Americans was not being taken very seriously.

He wanted to know where the Russian troops were. I told him that we had come from Torgau and showed him on the map that the Russian troops were located 2 to 3 km east of the city, just beyond the Elbe. Because I had a good knowledge of the local area, I was asked by the American Lieutenant to get into the jeep with the Americans and act as a guide to where the Russians were at Torgau. I would have liked to do this because we had had a wonderful talk together and a good understanding had developed in just 20 minutes. In general, no animosity had developed against each other. I very deliberately thought it over and after first agreeing, I hesitated and then politely refused. I explained as best I could that I would rather stay with my company because I felt responsible for my men. I also had an uneasy feeling about riding in an American jeep with the war still on. After a friendly "Good-bye", we parted company and the jeep headed in the direction of Torgau. We moved further through Oranienbaum.

Here we received a dispatch that we were to go to a farm house about 2 km from Oranienbaum for our noon meal. The food was still in the kettle when the guard at the gate notified us 2 American soldiers had arrived. I responded to shouts from them and was invited to go with them to their commander. There I saw to my astonishment that in the last half hour the place had been occupied by American troops. I smiled and called out, "The war is over". Then I was introduced to Captain Ewald, who told me in perfect German that our battle Commander, Major Freiherr von Schlotheim, had handed over his troops and was assured that we would not be given over to the Russians. I was instructed to bring all our weapons, gas masks, and helmets to a collecting depot. Everything went smoothly. After stacking our gear, we were able to eat our midday-meal.

Then we were given orders to move my company in the direction of the Mulde River. I was pleased and quite surprised to be trusted to move my men without any escort from the Americans. Surrendering to the Germans would never have been handled in the casual friendly manner of the Americans. Arriving at the Mulde Bridge of Raguhn, we were greeted by the Americans and given notice in a very rough tone that we were prisoners of war. At last, we were officially imprisoned by the Americans.

From here we were taken by several large trucks to a little camp near Eisleben. Then after 2 days we went into the big assembly camp at Bad-Kreuznach by train. The camp was in the open air and divided into many little camps. Altogether it held 100,000 prisoners. Officers were separated from the enlisted men. The food was very good but it was so scarce that we were often quite hungry. The first loaf of white bread, for example, was shared by 40 men. For bad weather, I had taken into captivity with me a tent-tarpaulin and that proved to be a good idea. I found 3 comrades with tent-tarpaulins and so we were able to make ourselves one tent out of these. The administration of the American camp explained to us that the German army was to blame for much of the bad conditions because many of the supplies had been destroyed during our retreat.

After about 3 weeks, we were taken to a very tidy camp for officers at St. Avold in Elsass-Lothringen. Here, there was a regular mess-hall with warm food and beverages. The German camp guide organized daily lectures to guard against boredom. These were kept fresh by professors and experts. The winter-months up to my dismissal in January 1946 were spent in the American separation center of Attichy near Reims. Here we also met the discharged prisoners from America who were taken there before 1945. The first release list was put together in the middle of January 1946 for transportation into the Russian personnel-zone for dismissal. I was included. We received our dismissal papers from the camp authorities and an envelope with our valuables (watch, money, etc.) that we had handed in at the time of capture.

I was in high spirits as I went by train over the Rhine River and crosswise through Germany, finally arriving at the Russian border zone. At the railway station in Eisenach, there was a welcoming-speech from a German official who presented only promises and falsehoods; for example, "Tomorrow you will be at home with your relatives and no longer treated badly as by the Americans and will be free individuals."

The trip soon continued to Erfurt where the release was to take place. As we came into a camp with huts, we submitted our dismissal papers which were then recorded. The next morning, we were accompanied by armed Russian soldiers to the railway station and went by "special-train" into the former concentration camp, Sachsenhausen. Political prisoners had already been imprisoned here. For us, a bad imprisonment began. We were placed in a hut-camp behind high walls with high-voltage barbed wire. All officers up to the level of colonel that were discharged from western prisons were here. We had to lie on wooden plank-beds with neither mattresses nor straw. An officer from Bad Liebenwerda that I had met in Camp Attichy came with a later shipment. He told us that the Americans in Attichy had warned him before dismissal not to drive into the Russian zone because the Russians did not release officers, but imprisoned them again. It was recommended that we remain in the camps and wait for release to the English or French zones.

This warning was ignored by a lot of people because everyone wanted to go home as quickly as possible.

By August of 1946, as the camp became overcrowded with 18,000 to 20,000 former German officers, they investigated us. All officers up to captain who were capable of work, regardless of age, were transported in small groups and under heavy security to Frankfurt/Oder. I do not know what happened to the staff- officers.

In Frankfurt/Oder, our hair was shaved off and we retained this polished look until shortly before our release in 1949. After a 2 day lay-over in Frankfurt/Oder, our group of about 400 men were taken to the railway station under strong guard. That was about the middle of July 1946.

Twenty-four men were placed in each boxcar containing only wooden planks. The cars were always firmly locked and were only opened for the issuance of food. The exhausting journey during the heat of the summer lasted about 3 weeks and took us through Poland, the Ukraine, and into the Caucasus. We were only fed once a day: 1 ladle of barley broth, 2 slices of dry bread and a cup of tea or malt-coffee. In addition, we feared for our futures because we knew the Russians had shot 15,000 Polish officers in Katyn.

From the autumn of 1946 until October of 1949, we had to perform hard work in various camps on the Black Sea coast. We often went for weeks without a day of rest. We constructed streets that led into mining and railroad-routes that went into the agricultural communes.

Finally, after over 4 years in captivity, I arrived in my country on November 4, 1949. During this long captivity, I often thought about the encounter with the American reconnaissance patrol in Oranienbaum on April 25, 1945, and asked myself, "How would my captivity have turned out if I had joined the Americans in their jeep to Torgau?".

In March of 1985, the celebration for the 40th Anniversary of the Link-up on the Elbe was announced. I read in my hometown newspaper that on April 25, 1985, Bill Robertson, the first American officer to meet the Russians in Torgau, would be present. So, I wanted to contact him to discuss events and went to the City of Torgau regarding my desire and to get suitable advice for making contact with him. To my surprise, I received a very gruff lecture that not every x#*#-GDR citizen could meet with the Americans. I did not know then that Bill Robertson was not the only person who led a patrol on April 25, 1945. From the book "Yanks Meet Reds – Encounter on the Elbe", I found out that several reconnaissance groups traveled in the direction of the Elbe. Maybe I will succeed during the 50th Anniversary in finding out which group I met in Oranienbaum in 1945.

ACROSS THE NIGHT SKY

by Delbert E. Philpott
271st Regiment, Co. A.,
69th Infantry Division

(*Editors Note*: The orginal title of this story, *Now When I Look Up At A Bright Dot Moving Across The Night Sky I Know The Spirit Of The Elbe Is Alive And Well*, has been edited for space considerations.)

The calendar shows that it is almost 50 years since our link-up on the Elbe River and I now reflect on how that event has affected my life. I wasn't able to return to the Torgau area until 45 years after our emotional and historic meeting. Standing on the banks of the Elbe River brought back a flood of personal memories.

Things have a way of changing over time and our reunion site is no exception. Most of us veterans remember our personal interactions during the link-up far better than the physical locations. Trees grow up, buildings are moved or built and war damage, including the bridges, is repaired. Normal civilian life has also returned. It's no wonder we often stand in a certain location and struggle with our memories.

The link-up and association with the Russian 58th Guards created a lasting impression which was beneficial to me in later years. As the propaganda of the Cold War divided us, I always remembered the warmth and friendship of the Torgau event. I was sure the average citizens did not hate each other.

I'm sure my first meeting with the Russians in 1945 was different from that of any other soldier. Indeed, my very first moment produced great personal relief. Before I had identified the distant soldiers as Russians, I had thought the mechanized column appearing on the other side of the river was German. This was due to the lack of Russian markings and their use of captured German vehicles. The realization that I wouldn't be captured while bringing back German prisoners was monumental. That unforgettable day started out quite innocently.

A close buddy had just returned from the hospital and was without souvenirs. He pleaded, cajoled and offered bribes to interest me in joining him for a walk to our outpost. He had heard Germans were giving up and wanted some tangible war booty to take home. From there he convinced me to hike beyond our lines. We came to a large river and followed it to the right for a long time. When at last we headed back, I noticed a German soldier cautiously standing up on a small embankment to our left. It was sobering to realize he had been in that area when we had passed much earlier and could have shot us. As I watched, he slowly raised his gun over his head and tossed it as far as possible. Then, he carefully walked down to us.

After I searched him, I explained in German that the war was over and said, "Let's go." To my amazement, he shook his head no. Looking at my loaded gun, he quickly pointed at his previous position. The hair stood up on the back of my neck. More Germans raised up from the weeds and grass, pitched their rifles and walked toward us. It was obvious that they would have killed us if we had harmed the soldier who had offered to be the one to test the safety of surrendering.

As we headed back, I had to endure the exuberance of my buddy, listening to his plans to write home about this event. However, this long march did seem worthwhile until I heard a motorized column on the other side of the river. Knowing it could be German as well as Russian, I made our prisoners lay down in a shallow ditch and covered them with a few branches. Gazing through my freshly obtained binoculars, I watched as the column came into view. The first trucks were unmarked, but the fourth was a German half-track. To this day I clearly see the dents and chipped paint making up the black German cross on its side. With their speed, we were being cut off and indeed could soon be prisoners of our prisoners. Not an enviable position to be in.

I watched from higher ground as the column disappeared along the river. I knew we had Americans at the bridge and decided to wait until the column reached that location. I told myself that if there was shooting, they were German - if not they should be Russian. That was my only hope.

I waited, straining to see with the binoculars. After what seemed an eternity I heard distant sounds of shooting. My heart sank. Germans! I strained to verify their identity once more as I refocused the binoculars. The distance was too great to see anything at ground level, but all of a sudden I could see objects in the air. Further observation and refocusing revealed these objects to be helmets. Greatly relieved, I shouted to my buddy, "It's a Russian column!"

We literally ran the entire distance back to the bridge area. No one was more sincere than I when I hugged, kissed and welcomed the Russians.

Our souvenir hunting had resulted in prisoners who could have shot us as we passed them and in being behind a motorized column that cut us off from our own troops. Luckily the column was an Allied one. Our letters home now added another adventure.

In 1990, our 45th reunion banquet with our Russian comrades was held in Leipzig. While looking at each others' photographs from 1945, I suddenly looked up at Anna Fominichna Tchuikova and quickly remarked on how strikingly similar her photograph was to the Russian lady who had given me my first hug and kiss. Before I knew what was happening, she grabbed me in a bear hug, swung me around 180 degrees while planting a kiss, and then slammed me back onto terra firma. Everything was identical to that first encounter in 1945. With my ears ringing and my ribs almost crushed I could only gasp, "You MUST be the lady; the first Russian soldier who greeted me!" The only thing changed was the date. I later had the pleasure of helping place a wreath at the tomb of the unknown soldier in Moscow and having my picture taken with her at that location (see photo).

Delbert E. Philpott and Anna F. Tchuikova standing beside the eternal flame at the tomb of the Unknown Soldier in Moscow, 1990. (Photo by D. A. Philpott)

During our extended 1945 celebrations, 2 Army Piper Cubs circled and landed in our area. Allan Jackson, a U.P. Army photographer was in one and Ann Stringer, a war correspondent, was in the other. They were looking for a link-up story. After photographing generals on both sides and other VIP's, Allan decided to create a backup picture by assembling a few American and Russian soldiers shaking hands to symbolize the link-up. We were posed by some debris with a damaged bridge in the background. We reached our hands out toward each other and Allan said, "Look at each other." The guy on my right looked at Allan just as he snapped the picture. Allan mumbled something under his breath, repeated where to look and took another photo. Thus, 2 pictures exist. The second photo also shows the four Russians more clearly because the fourth Russian was almost hidden behind the third one in the first picture.

Delbert E. Philpott (left) and Allan Jackson (right) at their reunion in 1991, reenacting the pose of his famous picture. (Photo by D. A. Philpott)

I learned later that Ann Stringer offered to take the film and see if she could make it back to Paris to deliver Allan's film while filing her story. Speed was vitally important as other correspondents were also trying to rush into print. When the pilot of the tiny two-place plane she was in spotted a C-47 landing in a grassy makeshift airfield, they landed by it. At first the C-47 pilot refused to believe that she had been at the link-up, but when he saw her typing her story she was flown on to Paris. As a result, her story and one of the link-up photos appeared in newspapers around the world. Some people call it the second most famous picture of World War II because it symbolized splitting Germany in half and signaled the certain end of a bloody, senseless and terrible war with Germany.

However, the war was still on and there were no newspapers, radios or direct information for us. Consequently, none of us saw the pictures or the article. In fact, everyone who had a camera was taking or posing for pictures. So posing for anyone quickly became quite routine modified somewhat by the quantities of Russian vodka we were consuming. Also, we knew nothing about what the reporters did once they quickly left our area. We existed on rumors and word-of-mouth-news. We still had to carry our loaded guns, but the euphoria of knowing there weren't any Germans in front of us and that we would live out the war was enough to completely occupy our minds. We could now do the unthinkable — plan on going home.

Two years went by before anyone in our group spotted the photo in Compton's Picture Encyclopedia. I didn't learn about the discovery until 30 years later. We feel it represents Company A and the spirit our Captain Austin imbued in all of us. The fact that a few of us were privileged to be in the picture is wonderful, but incidental.

In the early 1970's, I asked our government to offer space to Russian scientists on a gigantic balloon I was planning to fly from the magnetic north pole. This was to prevent any problems if our balloon drifted over Russia. Indeed, I was afraid that an unidentified balloon would be shot down and possibly cause an international incident. Because of this proposal, the Russians countered by offering us a place on their Cosmos 782 spacecraft. They correctly pointed out that their satellite would be better because the balloon flight could not be controlled. I was delighted when our government accepted their offer. Thus, the cooperation between the space programs of our 2 counties began with our mutual desire to put experiments into space in order to make space travel safe for humans. This proved to be a real stepping-stone in our relations with Russia.

I flew to Moscow and interacted with the Russian Space program. When they learned I had participated in the 1945 link-up and recalled that our two agencies had conducted the Apollo-Soyuz link-up in space in 1975, I was treated like a hero for a second time. They said I was the only person they had ever met who had participated in both link-ups between our two countries.

I then learned that the joint docking of the Apollo and Soyuz spacecrafts had occurred over the area of our historic 1945 link-up. This was accomplished at the request of the Russians. They reasoned that this was an appropriate opportunity to commemorate the first link-up of 1945. Sadly, our news media gave very little publicity to the importance of the gesture and the location for this memorable activity.

While in Moscow, I carried out my experiments and later returned with space-flown samples that other American scientists were eagerly awaiting.

The cooperation, exchange of information and progress we made towards safe space flight provided an activity for the politicians on both sides to observe. Six of my experiments and many other American experiments have since been flown on Russian spacecraft. Russian experiments are being flown on the American Shuttle flights.

During the latter years of the Cold War, our cooperation in space provided an example of success through mutual activity for a common goal. If I can ever be remembered for anything, I would like to be remembered for my initial part in developing the interaction in space between our two great countries. Now, Astronauts and Cosmonauts are flying on each other's spacecraft. When I look up at a bright dot passing overhead in the night sky I know the spirit of the Elbe is alive and well.

The first of two of Allan Jackson's link-up pictures. (L to R): Pfc. John A. Metzger, Delbert E. Philpott and Pvt. Thomas B. Summers; all from Co. A, 271st Regiment. Attempts to identify the 58th Guards Russians through the Red Star *newspaper have been unsuccessful. (Photo by A. Jackson)*

AS A YOUNG GIRL, I VOLUNTEERED TO GO TO WAR

by Anna F. Tchuikova
(Translation and adaptation by M. Bukhankova and D. Philpott)

I, Anna F. Tchuikova, am from the family of Marshal Tchuikov and am a World War II Veteran, with a disability of the 2nd group. I am alone now. My husband, the brother of Marshall Tchuikov, has died. As a member of the 8th Rifleman Division, I participated in the defense of Moscow and later became part of the 15th Tanks Division of Taman. (It is now the 2nd Division of Taman.)

As a young girl, I volunteered to go to war. I participated in the Battle of Stalingrad, the march to Berlin and in taking the Reistag. I was wounded several times and consequently, awarded with 12 orders and medals.

I was ready to give my life because of my feeling of devotion to the cause of freedom and to my people and my country. With these thoughts, I withstood the entire war until victory and the meeting on the Elbe on April 25, 1945. The international way of thinking was for other countries – not for us. We were just glad we won and were glad to meet the Americans. We transported them across the river and I gave flowers to some of the soldiers. After that was dancing, music, and celebrating.

Anna F. Tchuikova in 1945. (Photo provided by A. F. Tchijkova)

Our heart needs very few things – freedom, friendship and victory. I will remember this meeting for the rest of my life.

War is a terrible thing. We all shared the same ideas of independance for our nations and of peace and calm for everyone on earth. Thousands of our daughters and sons demonstrated their heroism in the fight against fascism. They were all heros because deep in their hearts they fought for the right cause. Together we won. People will never forget the battles for the honor and independance of our countries. We bow our heads low to the memory of those who died in the battles before the hour of victory. The honored remains of those who died in battle – American soldiers and officers and our soldiers and officers – and those who today are alive will celebrate the 50th Anniversary and freedom of the people of all nations.

This meeting on the Elbe April 25, 1945, will always be in the

Anna F. Tchuikova and other Russians greeting American GI's coming up the bank of the Elbe River. (Photo provided by A. F. Tchijkova)

memory of those who were tested by the terrors and horrors of war. When the veterans of our countries see each other in 1995, we won't forget our elbow to elbow

Anna F. Tchuikova placing a flower at the base of the monument in Torgau. (Photo provided by A. F. Tchuikova)

friendship and mutual aid. The 25th of April 1995, the veterans of our countries will meet at the Elbe. I will gladly participate and will give flowers like before and celebrate the victory. We will shake hands like in 1945 when the Americans crossed the river to our side of the Elbe. The joy of the meeting and sincere friendship of the citizens of America and the Soviet Union still remains through this time.

Anna F. Tchuikova is congratulated by a Russian General at a meeting of the regiment in April 1991. (Photo provided by A. F. Tchuikova)

HALT! UNLOAD GUNS! DON'T FIRE!
THERE ARE ALLIES IN FRONT OF US!

Dedicated to the 45th Anniversary of the
Meeting at the Elbe

by R. Agrikov,
Colonel in Retirement,
Candidate of Military Science
April 15, 1990 - Odessa

Editor's Note: R. Agrikov gave William Beswick this material in 1990, and he provided it for this book. Although it had already been translated into English, additional editing was necessary.

It's known that the meeting with our former allies, the Americans, took place in the combat zone of the 5th Guards Army of the First Ukrainian Front during the Berlin operation.

I had the luck of being a witness and a participant of the historic meeting of the anti-Hitler coalition of the two allied armies.

As it became known later, the Americans were supposed to stop at the border of the Mulde River, 30-40 kilometers to the west from the Elbe. But that didn't occur. Striving to occupy as much territory as possible, the allies moved forward up to the border of the Elbe without informing our headquarters.

Being a commander of the Regiment Artillery group, I directed the artillery formations commanders to survey probable river crossing points.

At about half of a kilometer from the riverbank, our captured "Opel" pickup was fired on by artillery from the opposite side. We had to leave the car and walk to the dam. Luckily, there were no casualties among the group. Reaching the dam, we quickly prepared the portable radio station for operation. The "to combat!" command was transmitted.

Responding to the firing, we carried on the combat for 40 minutes. After that, Michail Markitanov, reconnaissance man of the battalion control platoon, reported:

"The fascists hung out a white flag on the Riesa town fortress wall!"

Using field glasses, I really saw the flag, but it was not white and not a German one. I stopped the firing and reported by radio in a loud voice:

"I see a flag on the fortress wall, but it isn't the German one. I request instructions".

After that, I received the order of Colonel L. V. Zapolsky: "Stop firing until clarification!"

After 10 - 12 minutes, one more order appeared: "Halt! Unload guns! Don't fire! - There are allies in front of us!"

This occurred at midday on April 25, 1945. At that moment, I was possessed with mixed feelings of joy and responsibility. But soon all of us were overcome with delight. Soldiers and officers went to the dam, throwing up their garrison caps and field caps. "Hurrah" sounds came through. Flares of all colors were launched. Approximately the same scene was seen on the opposite bank.

On the left flank, soldiers were involved in fierce combat in our direction against the counter-attacking fascist troops. The units repelling the enemy's counter-attack were from the Polish Army and the 32nd Guards Rifle Corps of the 5th Guards Army. As later became known, some units of the allied American Army were engaged in the same action and also conducted combat against the fascists.

So up to this time, it is unknown whose artillery shelled us and against whose we had responded. The situation was extremely incomprehensible. It is no wonder neither side asserted claims either at the moment of the meeting or later. The war paid off everything, including the lack of necessary coordination between the allied armies. It seems clearly evident that we and the Americans, as real allies, should have had to exchange liaison missions at the proper time.

Actually, it is known that on April 25, 1945, at 16:40, in the combat zone of General Rusakov's 58th Guards Rifle Division, a reconnaissance group met a group of servicemen headed by Second Lieutenant William D. Robertson of the 69th U.S. Infantry Division at 40 kilometers to the northwest of Riesa near Torgau.

The Americans shouted: "America! Russia! Comrade! Comrade! Don't fire. There are allies here. There are Americans here! Moscow - America!"

Using a bridge in Torgau that was still somewhat intact, a man came from the west bank and soon Soviet soldiers embraced him. They shook hands with the reconnaissance officer of the First Battalion of the 273rd Infantry Regiment of the 69th Infantry Division, William D. Robertson. He was a future medical professor of the University of California in Los Angeles and owner of the Soviet Order of Alexander Nevsky.

Very few people know that there were other contacts. Only our 15th Guards Infantry Division led by General Chirkov reached the Elbe River on a front of approximately 30 kilometers. It was the first to cross the river near Riesa and, to the south of it, capture the bridgehead on the western bank. The 50th Guards Infantry Regiment of this Division, under the command of Major V. I. Medvedev, was one of those that contacted the Americans. The advance guard of this regiment reached the Elbe 24 hours earlier.

Following it was the advance guard of the 44th Guards Infantry Regiment led by Lieutenant-Colonel S. K. Gutsaluk. The 47th Guards Infantry Regiment, pursuing the enemy and acting as the division left flank guard, seized Grossenhein and kept it under control for 24 hours until the arrival of the division's main force. It had repulsed many counterattacks of the enemy.

We direct participants of the meeting didn't completely realize the meaning of the event. It was considered that the main affairs were occurring to the north in Berlin where a rugged battle was taking place.

The situation was defined by I. S. Konev, who wrote in his memoirs called "The Forty-fifth", as follows: "As we can see, the day of April twenty-fifth was full of great events. But the greatest occurred not in Berlin, but at the Elbe in the 5th Guards Army of General Zhadov, where the 34th Guards Corps of General Baklanov met with American troops. Exactly here in the center of Germany, Hitler's Army was finally cut in two pieces."

I want to quote a short extract from the report which we sent to the Stavka (The Commander-In-Chief's main organization): "April 25, 1945, at 13:30 in the zone of operations of the 5th Army near Strehla on the Elbe River, units of the 58th Division met the reconnaissance group of 69th Infantry Division of the 5th Army Corps of the 1st U.S. Army. During the same day near Torgau on the Elbe, the First Echelon Battalion of the 173rd Guards Infantry Regiment of the same division met another reconnaissance group of the 69th Division of the 5th Army Corps of the 1st U.S. Army."

Subsequently, the rank principle was kept. Regiment commander of the 58th Guards Infantry Division, Major Rogov, met with Charles Adams, the regiment commander of the 69th U.S. Infantry Division.

Then, General V. Rusakov, 58th Guards Rifle Division commander, met General E. Reinhardt, U.S. 69th Infantry Division commander, his staff officers and journalists.

Roman Agrikov—Odessa. (Photo provided by W. Beswick (photo given to Beswick by Agrikov))

The Americans were more than relaxed. There was an exchange of souvenirs, shaking of hands, laughing, etc. The soldiers had made contact very successfully. The American general presented General Rusakov with the state flag, but there was no gift in response.

On April 27, there was a meeting of the commander of the 34th Guards Corps, Baklanov, with the commander of the 5th Army Corps, Major General Huebner. Baklanov handed Huebner a red flag and the "Stalingrad Defense" medal. It was a symbol of our victories at the bank of the great Russian river, the Volga. It was a reminder of the victory over fascism and of the combat soldiers' friendship between our two nations. It took place in the presence of a clamorous group of journalists. Our side was represented by journalists Konstantin Simonov and Alexander Krivitsky. The talk was about Huebner's corps which had broken through France, Belgium, and Germany and since July 1944, had gone through nearly 1,100 kilometers in combat. Baklanov's divisions had gone through 2,250 kilometers in combat, from Stalingrad at the Volga to the Elbe. And there was the long-awaited meeting.

Roman Agrikov—photo taken in 1990. (Photo provided by W. Beswick (Photo was given to Beswick by Agrikov))

The meeting ended at the village of Werdau which is 5 kilometers from the river crossing point. Ukrainian borsch and Russian ravioli was prepared for 40 to 50 men of both sides. Everybody admired each other. There were toasts for meeting, victory, the friendship of the allied armies, for the prosperity of our people, for good luck, and for this war to be the last one. The leave-taking was very warm. They left with wild flowers. "Willis" jeeps were driven by our drivers because the American drivers liked our "vodka" too much. General Baklanov preferred this variant also.

The next day, General Baklanov met General C. Hodges, the Commander-In-Chief of the 1st U.S. Army, and accompanied him to the army residence of General Zhadov, the Commander-In-Chief of the

5th Guards. This was situated 30 kilometers from the Torgau River crossing point.

For the meeting of the two commanders, a big estate with a rather spacious house was chosen. General Hodge's suite was bigger than that of General Huebner. The journalists came in full strength.

On April 29th, Army General Petrov, the 1st Ukrainian Front Chief-Of-Staff, received General O. Bradley, the 12th Army group of troops' commander, the representative of the U.S. military elite. General Baklanov accompanied them to the residence of Marshal I. Konev.

Benevolence, admiration of the deeds of our Army and our people were very characteristic for all the meetings with the Americans. I was an eye-witness of it just after the ending of the war when our troops were located near Prague and maintained the demarcation line with the U.S. Army.

As our Commander-In-Chief, General Zhadov remembered his contacts with the Americans started on April 30, after the destruction of the Berlin grouping which launched the counter-attack against the army's left flank: "We spent the 30th of April together with the 1st U.S. Army commander, General Hodges. In a large, elaborately decorated hall, General Hodges and I told each other in a few words about the combat experience our armies gained during the war and remembered in our speeches those who had given their lives. Hodges and other American generals admired the strength of our troops in defense, the scale of the operation, and our high speed during the offensive operations. Among other questions, our guests were interested in the role of the help that was given to the Soviet Union by the United States during the war. Particularly, they asked about American weapons and vehicles which had been delivered for our 5th Guards Army. We told them frankly that in 1942, our army received a certain number of "Valentine" and "Churchill" tanks and heavy anti-aircraft weapons. But mainly, during the war, troops of the army were receiving weapons and vehicles of Soviet production. At the same time, we told them frankly about the important help from the American people which we received with a great amount of vehicles such as "Dodges","Willis",and especially "Studebakers". The last ones showed brilliant characteristics on war roads. For all this, we said "Thank You" to the Americans on behalf of our soldiers.

At the end of the meeting, General Hodges gave us a flag standard while saying: "I present it to the Russian 5th Guards Army. We carried this banner from America across the Atlantic Ocean, the English Channel, Normandy, France, and to Germany where we have met on the Elbe. Handing the standard to you, I give you and all the officers of your army my love and respect.."

I expressed to General Hodges my gratitude for his kind words toward the Soviet Army and added as follows: "On this long-awaited and happy day, we are full of joy for our nations and for our glorious soldiers. The heroic Soviet Army has passed through a great, hard and victorious war and is finishing it together with our allies by defeating fascist Germany completely. Let this meeting be the pledge of building a strong and lasting peace on our planet!"

We accompanied the guests up to the river. General Hodges invited us to join him. But soon troops of the 5th Army had to participate in the operation of defeating the group of armies of Field-Marshal Sherner and in liberating the central part of Czechoslovakia. That is why the second meeting with the generals, officers, and soldiers of the 1st U.S. Army took place later in Leipzig when military decorations were given to Soviet servicemen awarded by the President of the United States and Americans awarded by the Soviet Government. The author of this writing is one of those 32 Soviet men from the 5th Guards Army who were decorated by the U.S. President.

The guns were quiet. The bombing stopped. The machine-guns weren't firing. Headquarters was busy with routine training. I became the Chief of Non-commissioned Officers' School which was located to the south of Prague. Suddenly, I was called to the Army Commander Zhadov. There were a lot of thoughts and suppositions. Why was I called? The rough manners of the commander were well-known.

- "Major, what about a drink?" was the first question.
- "I can drink, Comrade Commander."
- "Everybody can. How much can you?"
- "Somebody has denounced me as a drinker", I thought. "And if he is asking me 'How much?', it means that he knows everything and I shall not lie. I must tell him the truth".
- "About half a liter, Comrade Commander."
- "So, after that?"
- "Usually, it's okay. Sometimes after that, I happened to go to the regiment commander to report."
- "And how did it end?"
- "Good. He noticed nothing."
- "I think the regiment commander drinks more than you."
- "Not at all, Comrade Commander!"
- "And have you got a new uniform?"
- "All I have is on me. Nothing new."
- "Go to the logistics department and let them measure you. Then wait for orders."
- "Yes".

Here the conversation reached the end. In seven to ten days, the call came. The Commander of the Division, General P. M. Chirkov, told us that a meeting with the Americans was expected. All of us were to put on all our military decorations. Among those who were to go were the Division Commander, the Division Chief-Of-Staff, V. E. Honicman, 50th Regiment Commander, V. I. Medvedev, Lieutenant A. D. Lovchikov, our famous sniper F. S. Sherotiuk, and me.

At army headquarters, each of us received an official car and driver. A column of 32 cars started from Prague to Leipzig. At the head of the column were chiefs of the army led by A. S. Zhadov. The distance was approximately 400 kilometers. We crossed the border of Czechoslovakia and entered Germany. Sometimes the column stopped. We spoke only about what was going to happen. Everybody realized the importance of the moment.

At last our column reached the river. Near the bridge, which was 10 to 12 kilometers from Leipzig, we were met by an American officer. He greeted us and led us into the city. When the army commander's car passed the bridge, it was immediately followed by a "Willis" with two machine-gunners on it. Then another of our cars went and another "Willis" and so on for each of our 32 cars. This is the way the escort of honor was formed.

By the time we entered the city, there were 64 cars in the column. We couldn't fail to notice that there were traffic regulators on each road intersection, anti-air-craft machine-guns on each corner of the street, and the streets were free of citizens.

When we reached the central square, we saw troops prepared for a parade and a raised platform. Having parked the cars and shaken off the road dust, we gathered in front of the platform.

Soon the "Call to Attention" order was transmitted, national anthems of the Soviet Union and the U.S.A. were performed and the decoration ceremony began. First they announced the names of those who were receiving awards from the President. We responded "Me". The army commander, General Hodges, being accompanied by an aide who carried the decorations, approached each person being rewarded, and pinned the order above the Soviet ones. After that, he shook hands with each of us while we responded: "I serve the Soviet Union!" - trying to shout loudly and to be heard throughout the whole square.

I was unexpectedly surprised when I heard my name (Agrikov) spoken with the stress placed on the fourth letter.

Having pinned the "Legion of Honor" to my chest, General Hodges continued to the next person. At the same time, I followed my comrades by rearranging the American decoration below the Soviet ones. Colonel-General Zhadov was awarded "The First Grade Commander".

After the decoration ceremony, the American troops of the Leipzig region marched in a parade to honor us. Then in one of the best restaurants of the city, a reception took place with 80 generals and officers from the American side and 32 from ours. There also were non-commissioned officers among us.

During the parade, I noticed that the uniforms of the soldiers and junior and senior officers were the same. The difference was in the quality of material. The color and the pattern was the same.

We were dispersed inside the restaurant. I was surrounded by a colonel and two lieutenant-colonels. One of them introduced himself as the army corps intelligence officer. The commanders occupied a long square table against the front wall in the center of the hall. Other tables were round. The reception began with a greeting speech by General Hodges. He proposed a toast: "Lets raise our glasses to the victory over our mutual enemy - fascism - and to the glorious Russian Army.

A toast in response was proposed by A. S. Zhadov: "Let's raise our glasses to the long-awaited meeting of the two allied armies", - and he expressed his hope that our nations would do their best to preserve peace. The toast was received with agreement. We shook hands with each other, embraced, and exchanged souvenirs. The colonel presented me with a little compass which I still keep as a precious souvenir. We exchanged addresses. We wrote our addresses on the occupation banknotes and this excited all the participants because it happened unexpectedly. I handed them a 10 crown note and received a German occupation mark and we began writing.

Spontaneous toasts began to happen. First we drank whisky. Then one of the Lieutenant-Colonels asked me:
- "How did you like our whisky, Major?"
- "It's rather good. It's worth drinking, but our vodka is better."
- "Vodka? We have vodka."
He called the waiter who was a German:

- "Bitte, vodka."
- "Jawaohl", he said, and went out. In two minutes, he
  was back carrying a one-liter bottle wrapped with a
  napkin. Opening the napkin with a showy manner, he put
  the bottle on the table.

  I saw that it was "Pshenichnaya" and asked: "Where did
  you get our vodka from?"
- "You traded actively with Germany before the war. We captured it in great
quantities in Danzig and other cities and ports," was the answer.

Taking the initiative, I proposed, "Gentlemen, let's drink Russian vodka in the
Russian manner. But we need big glasses for this."

The interpreter, the U.S. Army officer who was at our table, translated the sug-
gestion. The colonel called the waiter again and in a moment, four large glasses
appeared on our table.

I poured the drink in to the glasses, asked them to follow me and I drank the
contents of the glass completely. My companions excitedly reacted, but didn't follow me. It was too hard for them without experience, but they finally finished their
drinks.

Half an hour hadn't passed before vodka appeared on every table. It was also
on the commanders' table.

The speeches grew excited. They were about many items, but the greatest interest was shown towards the war with Japan. Particularly, the colonel asked me:
- "Mr. Major! When, in your opinion, will your army be
  ready to stand with us against Japan?"
- "Mr. Colonel, you should address your question to
  another authority. I'm just an artillery battalion
  commander. My unit is ready to fulfill the orders of
  the commanders anytime against any enemy."
- "We know well the combat abilities of your boys," - the
  colonel continued. - "We envy you Russian officers.
  You have got excellent material. Your boys do not demand
  much. They assault the machine guns. We can't say the
  same for ourselves. We have to bring beds for our
  soldiers. We prepare and conduct artillery and aviation
  firings for 3 - 4 hours. The assault begins and if there
  is even one undestroyed enemy machine gun, they lie there
  and no force will make them continue. We have to begin
  again. If you were equipped with our weapons, you could
  conquer the world."

Even now, I'm surprised how I could find an answer: "We don't want to
conquer the world. The people of the world will make it socialist by their own
hands. You noticed weapons, so we do have the strongest."

My companions became tense. It seems to me now that they thought that I
hinted at nuclear weapons about which I didn't know anything at that time. But
they knew something because the U.S.A. possessed the atomic bomb at that moment. But I evidently disappointed them, saying that the weapon was invented by
Marx, Engles, and Lenin.

- "You are a young diplomat all right. Bravo, Major!"

The reception lasted approximately 4 hours. A lot of things were spoken of and a lot of drinks were drunk. Our hosts became slow. At last, farewell toasts were said. General Zhadov invited the Americans to be our guests. The invitation was gratefully accepted. When our army commanders stood up, we followed them and shook hands, embraced, cut off buttons from our uniforms, and exchanged them. Many of the Americans liked our red stars very much. Only 12 - 15 men were able to accompany us to the cars. The others couldn't.

Our cars had been washed. Each was supplied with 1 - 2 full auxiliary fuel tanks. The column started back.

In 7 - 8 days, we accepted 32 guests led by General Hodges. Almost all of the generals and officers were acquainted. The reception lasted until morning. When the sun rose, we accompanied our guests up to their cars, but with our drivers because the Americans had overindulged themselves with the specially prepared delicacies. They were entertained by Captain Skliar, the aide of the corps commander, General Baklanov.

I remember the interpreter, later an aide of General Hodges - Michael from Petersburg - as he introduced himself in Leipzig.

He was the son of a Russian colonel from Petersburg. In 1917, the father took the family to Australia. Then they went to America. When the war began, the father told his sons to go to Europe and, together with the allied powers, help the Russians.

I asked him, "How old were you when you left Russia?"

The answer was, "I was two years old. My brothers were five and seven."

"Michael, how do you happen not to forget the language? You speak very clearly." - I asked him.

"It was thanks to my father. At home, we spoke only Russian. Outdoors, we spoke English, but as soon as we passed through the door, we spoke only Russian. He beat our lips if we forgot the rule. He loved the Motherland very much. All his life, he was very sad about it. He even built a Russian stove in the house. He is very proud of building it by himself. Mother is also a real Russian woman. As for me, only the shoulder-straps are American. I am wholly Russian..."

We exchanged addresses. Last time Michael came to see me in Austria at the end of 1946, I remember his sad words: "Roman, there is a cold wind blowing from the West from overseas. All those who fought together with you returned to the U.S.A. They didn't believe me, a Russian, and also didn't believe my Chief, General Hodges."

For obvious reasons, our contacts stopped. But I haven't lost hope in finding these people. At the same time, I realize that it won't be easy.

Contacts between our countries are gradually beginning to take shape, but in the Soviet Committee of War Veterans, the fact is that there are people who have direct involvement with events of 1945-46 who are not valued. We, the participants of the Elbe meeting, the owners of American decorations, are forgotten. Mostly, those who live in Moscow visit the United States, but they are always the same people. Often they weren't involved with the April 1945, meeting at all.

As the experience of meetings with Americans in the city of Odessa (where I live) shows, they become very easily influenced when then see an American decoration on a uniform. For instance: In 1987, I was invited by Intourist to a meeting with American Christian Church representatives. There were about 40 people. The conversation lasted about one and one half hours. The end was unusual. One of the nuns suddenly said:

- "Mr. Colonel, let me kiss you."
- "Are you not afraid," said I. "I'm a Communist."
- "That isn't the main thing. The main thing is that you were fighting against fascism with my father. He was killed in Europe. I want to kiss you as I kissed my father."

She was followed by 10 - 12 American women. Their eyes were bright with tears. My eyes also became wet.

The main subject of conversations was how to promote peace in the world. All of us agreed on one point: friendship among people is the pledge of success. No government can unleash a war if the people are against it. Peace and life are indivisible. There is no life without peace.

I made them remember that history records 14,500 wars which took 3,500,000,000 lives. If nature hadn't erased all the scars and graves of the victims of human madness, our little planet would have become a world of cemeteries.

"Down with wars! Long live peace on earth!" Vladimir Ilyich Lenin was the first who addressed their words to the whole world. The darkness of unfriendliness and the ghosts of war will be removed by friendship and peace if all of us, believers and atheists, little and big nations, unite and say a powerful NO TO WARS! The price of war is paid by tears and also by a mother's pain. Remember well forever all those who died. We don't want to permit war to be again."

Forty-five years have passed from the day of the meeting of the two armies on the Elbe and now we are called to Torgau again. The voice of American brothers-in-arms is received by us, the Soviet Veterans. Years, wounds, and sicknesses are not considered when the topic is peace.

On April 25, 1990, another Soviet and American war veterans' Elbe meeting will take place. It will take place to confirm that the Spirit of the Elbe cannot be annihilated. It will last forever. Our friendship which was born in the battlefield against the common enemy must illuminate the way of our great nations and must serve as an example for youth.

R. Agrikov, Colonel In Retirement,
Candidate of Military Science
April 15, 1990 - Odessa

THEY LIKED FRUIT COCKTAIL

by Roland Hendrickson
273rd Regiment, Co. D
69th Infantry Division

My involvement with the Russians occurred about mid-May. I was in Benewitz until mid-June. The Russians occupied Wurzen. The bridge for the main road was blown up and the Russians had built a small wooden bridge used to transport DP's (displaced persons) back to the Russian sector. POW's and DP's from the American sector came back to the American side.

The Russians counted every POW/DP and traded one for one. One day, there was a convoy going east and the Russians had a band playing at the Exchange Point. However, when the convoy returned with the Allied POW's and DP's, the band had left so everything came to a stop while the Russian officer in charge insisted that the band be returned for the west bound convoy.

We exchanged food and other items with the Russian soldiers. When a jeep brought food, the Russians on duty would come over for a visit. They LIKED fruit cocktail. Once they brought dark, coarse bread and a tasty chunk of bacon-type meat and, of course, vodka. We got to know the regular soldiers, but didn't get as well acquainted with the second group of Russians. The first group was more friendly.

Our group of 69th Infantry soldiers could hear celebrating in Wurzen, but none participated in the celebrations except one. He went over to visit one afternoon and didn't return until the next day with a very big hangover. Of course we could hear the accordion playing and singing far into the night. We used to take a target down by the river and exchanged weapons just to test for target practice. Once an M-1 rifle a Russian soldier was holding went off because he didn't know it was automatic and barely missed me. The soldier was very short, and with the butt of the rifle resting on the ground, bayonet attached, it was about 2 feet taller than he was. This was a comical sight. The Russians weren't supposed to cross the river, but sometimes did when they'd had too much vodka. The Americans had to turn them around and send them back.

I had a Russian flag which was given to me by some DP's. I took it to Leipzig in 1990 when we had our reunion banquet with the Russian Veterans and was told that the Russian lettering on it said "Long Live Stalin". Two Russians came over and signed it, but one became upset, though I don't know why. I was afraid it might cause an international incident, but things soon calmed down. Most communication between the Russian and American Veterans at the banquet was by means of gestures and bits of German. I have corresponded with a couple of the Veterans since then, but communication is limited, mostly due to the slow mail.

Other than these events, the initial contact with the Russian soldiers has impacted my life very little.

MEETING AT THE ELBE

by Leonid Zilberberg
9th Tank Brigade,
U.S.S.R. Army

I was born in 1923 and joined the Army in 1941. I served in the Medical Corps assigned to the 9th tank brigade and held the rank of Lieutenant when we met on the Elbe River. I remained in the Army after the war and retired in 1975 as a Lieutenant Colonel.

Near the end of April, 1945, our 13th Army came up to the Elbe River. On April 27, 1945, our Supreme Commander-in Chief #379 expressed his appreciation to our Detachment for capturing Wittenberg. This was an important strong point in the defense of the Elbe. I still have as one of my prized possessions this charter which he issued.

One virtue that everyone seems to possess is forgetting events of the past. However, some events cannot be forgotten. I spent the whole war being first in Europe and then in Japan. Even though al-

Leonid Zilberberg at age 22. (Photo provided by L. Zilberberg)

most 50 years have passed and I have forgotten many events, it is impossible to forget our memorable meeting with the American soldiers on the Elbe in the city of Torgau.

We were told the American troops were moving eastwards towards the Elbe River. The retreating German Fascists unexpectedly appeared in front of us on our way west, but we overcame this opposition. We had been told the American ve-

Dr. Leonid Zilberberg, now retired from the Russian Army and living in the United States, 1994. (Photo by D. A. Philpott)

hicles would have white stars on their sides. We were happy to see the American troops moving towards the Elbe. At last they reached the city of Torgau which had been liberated the day before. Both sides were so happy to meet that we couldn't hide our tears as we kissed and put our arms around each other. That meeting meant the terrible war was over.

The American soldiers entertained us with their meals which seemed delicious to us and we gave them our traditional Russian meals. Wishing to please us, The American soldiers said, "Very good", but best of all they liked the Russian vodka. We didn't know the languages of each other but we understood each other because we were friends.

The young female traffic controllers in Torgau were at all the street crossings. The American soldiers delightfully watched them work. When the traffic stopped for a while, they would come up to the girls, tell them pleasant words and give them some chocolate. But we were not envious. We liked the gallantry of the American soldiers. We were quite surprised to see a lot of black soldiers who were treated equally with the white soldiers and how they respected each other. We remembered being told about the suppression of the black people in the U.S. and were curious about this, but we were not allowed to ask questions.

At that time in 1945, we didn't know that Stalin would begin the "Cold War" against our former allies. We didn't know that those people whom we had met on the Elbe and who had been our friends should be considered as enemies. At that time we didn't know that our historian-falsifiers would propagandize and falsely educate the younger generation by declaring that the Soviet Army had fought alone and by hiding the facts regarding the assistance of the United States and England. Stalin tried to make former friends appear to be our enemies, but we couldn't forget the American Studebakers, Fords, Dodges and Willies.

And now almost 50 years later, I'd like to say that the American people are as friendly as they were in April 1945. When the stranger in the street greets me with a friendly "Hi", and smiles at me, I remember that April in 1945, and the young American soldiers and it seems to me that I have become younger.

MEETING THE RUSSIANS

by Seymour C. Abrams
T/Sgt., 269th Engineers Combat Battalion, Co. C.,
69th Infantry Division

Meeting a few Russians from near the area where I was born - I believe it was the men of the First Ukrainian Russian Army - was an experience I will never forget. I realized then more than ever before that people are the same. They have the same wants and needs even though the government plants bad seeds about others whom we do not understand. The leaders are the culprits because of the differences in ideology. There was no hate, but rather camaraderie with the Russians. We exchanged gifts and guns or booty we had liberated. They

Seymour Abrams by the 69th Inf. Div. sign at the entrance to Leipzig in 1945. (Photo by S. Abrams)

were friendly towards us and had nothing but admiration for us. We, the 69th, captured Leipzig, but had to give it to the Russians because, I believe, it was planned prior to our occupation of the city by the higher echelon. The Russians admired our equipment, uniforms and food. Theirs was shabby in contrast, but I guess they had more than their families in wartime.

For future generations, I have a few thoughts I would like to pass on:

Realize that people love people no matter where you come from. Just be <u>kind, understanding, patient, honest and loving</u> . We all want peace to live our lives the best way we know how. We want love, comfort, to make a decent wage so we can support our families, and to be able to trust our neighbors and friends and respect other people's rights and beliefs as we would want them to respect ours.

Believe what is right to you and fight for it with dignity, with negotiation, arbitration, and through the ballot box – NEVER through war. War accomplishes nothing but more wars, more hatred, more despair, more pain. I hope and pray that there shall be no more war here or anywhere else in the world.

Editor's Note: Seymour was born near Odessa, in the town of Kirovgrad. At the age of 9, he came to the United States to be with an aunt and uncle who were already living here. They adopted Seymour, one brother, and two sisters as their own after learning that his mother, father, a sister, and

Seymour Abrams—retired. (Photo provided by S. Abrams)

two brothers had died from starvation. This was the time of the overthrow of the Czar in 1917. The Russian people were starving by the thousands. There was no government and they suffered from the lack of jobs.

He was raised in New Jersey and volunteered for the Army on August 4, 1943. After basic training in Camp Upton, New York, he was sent to Camp Claiborne, Louisiana, and Camp Shelby, Mississippi, before being transferred to Lathrope Engineering Depot in California for special assignments. More special assignments in California awaited him in Brea, Santa Anita (Prisoners of War), and Fort McArthur. He went from there to New York where he was shipped overseas.

Seymour's unit arrived in Southampton, England, on December 12, 1944, and was in La Havre, France, by January 21, 1945. They got as far as Leipzig in Germany. Other 69th Infantry Units went to the Elbe River where they linked up with the Russian Army's 58th Guards Division. Curiously, Russia's first Ukrainian Army to be met by the 69th Infantry Division was from the very same area where Seymour was born in 1914.

Although he's now retired from his real estate business, Seymour continues to keep his license active. He lives in southern California with a lady friend and actively participates in community and civic affairs. He is an active member of the Veterans of Foreign Wars.

MY RUSSIAN CONNECTION

by Robert L. Pierce
273rd Regiment, Co. I
69th Infantry Division

My earliest thoughts of Russians conjured up visions of poor peasant people struggling to survive after a long and bloody Revolution. Even when I first heard about the Russian Army during our "GI" orientation sessions, they were an abstract faction losing the war to Germany. The might and power of the Russian Army only became a reality when the 69th Division joined the three combat commands in a drive across Germany to split the Third Reich in half.

Stars and Stripes and our Officers were expounding the virtues of two famous Russians: Marshal Georgi Zhukov and Marshal Ivan Konev. Both Marshals were driving across Poland with approximately 750,000 soldiers each. Marshal Zhukov was the closest to Germany so our daily inquiries were "how close is Zhukov today?" His progress always brought cries of "Go Zhukov!" Marshal Konev then closed the gap and turned North to be in a position to attack Berlin before Marshal Zhukov could get there. We were told that Marshal Zhukov stopped all PX rations to the troops until they reached Berlin. This was an attempt to motivate his troops to fight harder to reach Berlin before Marshal Konev. We knew the Tri-Power's agreement gave the Soviet Government the right to take Berlin. Premier Joseph Stalin insisted on this position so the Russian Army could have the right to capture Berlin in retaliation for the destruction the Germany Army had made during the battles of Leningrad, Stalingrad, and Moscow.

Berlin became the "Grand Prize" for the first Russian Marshal who could capture it. Marshal Konev beat Marshal Zhukov into Berlin by a full day, but Stalin awarded the prize to Marshal Zhukov by placing the dividing line between the two Marshal armies so that the German Reichstag (the prize plum) was in Marshal Zhukov's area. The Russian drive to Berlin was critical to our own survival. We knew that as soon as the Russians attacked Berlin from the East, the Allied Forces would attack from the West and the war would be over. Our main interest was how soon would this happen? Would the war end before we fought our next battle? How many of us would still be alive to go home after the war ended?

Our main interest was more on the drive of the Russian Army to Berlin than on the eventual meeting between the 69th Infantry Division and the Russian Army. When we reached the Mulde River and heard the Russian Army was close to the Elbe River, we knew the war was almost over for us because the rivers were only 14 miles apart.

We were under strict orders not to cross the Mulde River but to wait for the Russian Army to reach us. While we waited at the Mulde River, patrols were sent each day to the Elbe River to see if the Russians had arrived.

The point we controlled was the bridge crossing of the Mulde River at Wurzen. The bridge was gone but it was possible to walk across the trestle of the bombed-out railroad bridge. There was a low irrigation dam in the river that diverted the water to one side and created a wide grassy area by the river bed. Orders were very specific: "Don't shoot unless attacked, affect the surrender of all German soldiers, let any Allied prisoners of war pass, but no civilians of any nationality." Displaced persons were later sent to Polenz Air Base for processing.

Our thoughts of what to expect from the Russian soldiers were magnified by the expressed fears of the German people, both civilian and military. They were terrified and convinced they were in mortal danger. The German people were attempting to completely evacuate the sector between the Mulde and Elbe Rivers to gain the sanctity of the American Army.

The plight of the German citizens was heart-rendering and pitiful. People were leaving their homes with only what they could carry on their backs or pull in their small hand carts. Everyone cried, begged and pleaded to be allowed to cross the River. Old men offered their wives to us; women offered themselves. There was even a couple who offered their 12-year old granddaughter if they could cross. The little girl was so terrified of being "caught" by the Russians that she not only agreed to having sex with us, but begged us to help her family. In all confidence, I can assure everyone that no sexual favors were accepted by the Americans at the bridge! I will confess that many bottles of wine and schnapps were given to us as a pure gesture of friendship and perhaps our protectorship when the Russians came; but no bridge passes!

(Left and middle) French Officer and liasion lady sent by the French Government to screen French POWs and DPs for eligibility to return to France as some French citizens had become collaborators. (Right) S/Sgt. Chester Ritchie, 2nd Platoon, Co. I, 273rd Regiment. (Photo provided by R. L. Pierce)

The sheer numbers of German soldiers surrendering to Co-I, 273rd Inf. at the Mulde was of such a magnitude it raised our anxiety and fears of what to expect from the Russians. Thousands of German soldiers still in full uniform and armed, surrendered. During the day there were soldiers coming down the road as far as the eye could see. As I recall, around 1500 to 2000 armed German soldiers surrendered in a three(3) day period. They still had the power to fight, but the will to fight was gone as the fear of being captured by the Russians was too over-powering.

Our orders were to remove their weapons and strip-search them. This meant they dropped their rifles in one pile, hand guns in another, dumped out any baggage they were carrying, emptied their pockets, and removed their clothes down to their underwear to assure there were no hidden weapons. As an American soldier, I am ashamed to say their possessions were summarily looted by scavenging American GI's. Anything of value was taken from them: cameras, medals, watches, rings, jewelry, coins, pocket knives, etc.

Russian guard at Wurzen in front of portraits of Lenin, Stalin and Churchill. (Photo provided by R. L. Pierce)

There were few if any complaints from the German soldiers. They were too grateful to be alive as an American prisoner.

The terror the German soldiers had for the Russians was exemplified by their total evacuation of a local German hospital. A German medical officer led a procession of broken-down wagons, a horse-drawn ambulance, and a long line of walking wounded. Nurses were assisting litter patients as they were being carried by the less disabled. Many hobbled with canes or walked on crutches. Those that could were half dragging, half carrying other wounded soldiers. The medical officer was very empathic. If the wounded were captured by the Russians, they would surely be killed or die of their wounds. He was convinced that only the Americans would provide his patients with medical care. The wounded were allowed to cross the broken bridge structure with the assistance of the American GI's.

When we got the news that Lt. Robertson's patrol had met the Russians at Torgau, it was the most exciting day in my life. I knew now the war in Germany was over for me

Two Russian displaced persons waiting to be exchanged so they can go home. (Photo provided by R. L. Pierce)

Russians arriving in Polenz, all packed and ready to be exchanged for repatriation, are shown moving a picture of Stalin. (Photo provided by R. L. Pierce)

and I was still alive. In all honesty, I must pause here to say: "No, I did not ever meet the Russians at the Elbe." In the past 49 years, I can hardly remember talking to another ex-69'er who did not meet the Russians someplace at the Elbe River. My first Russian connection came later on the West side of the Mulde River.

Co-I, 273rd was relieved at Wurzen and moved to a captured German Poison Gas and Ammo Dump outside the town of Altenhaim that had become a collection point for processing Allied prisoners of war. This area was only a couple of miles from Wurzen. One day three of us decided to walk down to see if the Russians had reached the Mulde yet. As we neared the river, we heard lots of screaming and hollering coming from a house in the small village there. The door was open so we entered to see who was killing whom. We had our first encounter with a Russian soldier. In fact, there were three of them. They were in the process of raping a young woman and attempting to strip an older lady. When we hollered at them to stop, someone started to shout and pound on a closed door. We opened the door to find the old lady's husband where the Russians had locked him up. The Russian

Two Russian women packed and waiting to be exchanged so they can go back to Russia. (Photo provided by R. L. Pierce)

soldiers were very happy to see us and even hugged us. Through sign language and gestures, they let us know it was OK for us to take our turn with the young woman before they finished. We convinced them to stop and gently but firmly escorted them from the house. They were not mad or upset. They were half drunk (although fully armed) and in a very happy frame of mind. My first encounter with a Russian soldier reinforced my previous fears and anxieties.

We continued to the river bank only to come under machine gun fire. We dropped down and crawled to the edge to see where all the shooting was coming from. Across the river on the lower grassy area were two Russian soldiers with automatic sub-machine guns firing at floating objects in the shallow river. Their bullets were ricocheting off the rocks in the river and flying all around where we were. We started yelling at them until they finally stopped. When we stood up, they recognized us as Americans and started yelling back and waving their arms. About that time, another object came floating by so they resumed shooting as before. We ducked down and moved out of range. My assessment based on these first two experiences was that the Russian rank-and-file soldier was an ignorant, childlessly simplistic and irresponsible person. My fears of what to expect had lessened; however, their actions made you want to be very cautious around them.

The Corp of Engineers built a wooden bridge across the railroad trestle at Wurzen. The Russian Army had armed guards posted on their side of the bridge, and a billboard with pictures of Lenin, Stalin, and Churchill. We had no guards on the American-occupied side. The bridge became the first outdoor shopping mall. The Russian Army had not been paid in about three years because of their economical situation. The U.S. Government, in addition to military and civilian aid, gave the Russian Government copies of the U.S. script mark plates so they could print American-backed currency to pay their military. Their script marks had a different series letter and a slightly lighter shade of color, but otherwise were interchangeable and as acceptable as the U.S. script mark. All the possessions looted from the German soldiers, souvenirs collected, and extra PX rations were sold by the American GI's to the Russians at the bridge. Money was no object. A Russian female officer opened a bandana that contained her three-year back pay of roughly $7,000 in script marks. Any pocket watch, whether it worked or not, sold for $50. I saw a Mickey Mouse watch sell for $350. Many GI's literally got rich at the bridge because the Russians had no sense of value at all and were loaded with currency. They didn't even understand the currency; only what the numbers meant. Since no one could converse in either language, all negotiations were by pencil. The American would write a number on the new lumber of the bridge. If the Russian disagreed, he would cross it out and write another number under it, and so on.

The Russian soldiers were very outgoing, friendly, and hospitable, offering to share whatever they had to drink. In those days, drinking was the second most important thing on a GI's mind. The first was against the law because it was a court martial offense to fraternize with the German girls. Communication between the Russian soldiers and ourselves was virtually impossible because of the language barrier. Even the Russians had several different country languages in their mix. Needless to say, no close friendships were made.

Our next assignment was at the German Polenz Air Force garrison outside Altenhaim. This huge facility became the East-Meets-West processing point for Allied prisoners of war and displaced persons from almost every country in Europe. From the West they arrived on foot, in trucks, and by train. The Russian displaced persons always decorated their vehicles with green pine boughs. I never understood why.

It's important to point out that the Russians soon became very possessive and demanding. They closed their river crossings to everyone except soldiers from English-speaking countries. The Russian border personnel insisted on an exchange of POW and DP's rather than opening the borders to whoever wanted to return to their native countries. This process delayed the exchange because every person had to be interrogated by both sides and sorted by nationality. When it became obvious that we had more Russian-displaced people than they had Western European people, they increased the ratio of exchange to insure they would get back all their people first.

On the Allied side, processing moved very rapidly to return POW's and DP's to the Western European countries. The French had their own Liaison group and interrogated every French soldier or civilian. They were looking for collaborators. During the war, the German Government had offered asylum to prisoners and displaced persons who would agree to become German citizens. This offer did not include Jews. Those that accepted were free to work in the German defense plants, marry, and live a free life as a German. Many European soldiers and displaced persons accepted this opportunity. When the war ended, they attempted to return by lying about their German citizenship. Most were caught because the other prisoners and displaced persons knew who they were and sought them out to turn them in as traitors.

Every day and every night was a party, especially for the people from the Soviet Union. They must have stolen every musical instrument in Germany when the war ended. There were even pianos with them. Life-size pictures of Lenin and Stalin were everywhere. With all the empty airport hangers and miles of runways, there was always room for another group to strike up the band and start dancing. Their confiscated German wine, beer, and schnapps flowed like water day and night.

While sorting out the different nationalities, we found many young girls with their red and white ribbons pinned on their clothes to signify that they were Polish. However, talking with them determined they were Polish Jews who had been masquerading as Polish. Apparently when the German Army was rounding up Polish laborers to ship to Germany, many of the younger people claimed to be Polish to escape a trip to the concentration camps.

The Russian civilians were the happiest and most cheerful people I have ever met. They didn't even appear to be mad at the Germans. In fact, many Russians became good friends with the German farmers they worked for during the war.

Exchange of prisoners and displaced persons ended near the end of June 1945. While we were processing the POW/DP personnel, the Division was also processing our personnel for return to the United States or to other units. When the last exchange was completed, we were a limited strength organization. Polenz Air Base was to be turned over to an advance Guard of the Russian Army and we were to be trucked West to what later became known as the "American Zone of Occupation".

My last connection with a Russian left a pang of fear in my heart and a lasting impression of people with a very hard-minded, possessive attitude. When we were leaving Polenz, our assigned unit trucks could not carry the remaining number of American soldiers. We had originally reached the Mulde River either by riding on tanks or in transportation trucking company vehicles. The Armored Divisions and trucking companies were long gone. This lack of transportation necessitated the use of the German Army trucks that were at the Polenz Ammo dump.

We loaded up the trucks and lined up in a convoy by Unit. Our Battalion Commander, Col. Leo W. Shaughnessy, was in the lead jeep and started to drive out of Polenz. The Russian Army Advance Guards were at the gate. There were several soldiers around the guard shack and one standing in the middle of the gate, blocking the way with his sub-machine gun at port arms. The Russian in charge was a junior officer who advised Col. Shaughnessy in English that we could not leave the compound with the German trucks because they were now Russian Government property. Col. Shaughnessy argued that he had no other way back to the U.S. Zone, but the Russian officer was very adamant. His orders were "no Russian property was to leave the area".

Col. Shaughnessy stood up in his jeep, turned around towards the first 2 1/2-ton truck behind him and shouted at the Lieutenant in the passenger's seat: "Load and man that 50". The lead truck had a 50 Cal. machine gun mounted in the ring mount with a full box of belted ammunition. The Lieutenant jumped up, loaded the gun and pointed it towards the Russian gate guard. Col. Shaughnessy looked at the Russian officer and very loudly said: "You have two choices. Either start shooting or stand aside." He turned to his driver and said "move" and at the same time gave the hand signal to advance. The guard stepped to one side and the Russians watched as our convoy drove out of Polenz.

THIS CLOSES THE RUSSIAN CHAPTER OF MY LIFE.

WE TOOK COVER WHEN THE HORSEMEN FIRED INTO THE AIR

as told by Dr. Arthur G. Seski, M.D.
Division Medical Inspector
69th Infantry Division

News of the link-up traveled fast. General Reinhardt was, of course, anxious to meet the Russians. A call came in from the General's location saying that he and the heads of his staff were preparing to immediately travel to the link-up location. As Division Medical Inspector, I was to be part of this entourage and gladly dropped everything so as to join the motorcade to the Elbe River.

I remember the weather as being warm and balmy, but the knowledge that no more casualties would be coming in would have made any day a wonderful one. Driving into Torgau, we were met by Russians at the river's edge. Here we were bundled into small narrow punts that looked like racing shells and the Russians rowed us through the rapidly-moving stream to the other side. My first impression as I glanced about could best be described as a group of straggling Russians using every type and form of transportation possible. Some were on foot, others were using horses, bicycles and occasionally we saw a "lend-lease" jeep. These were occupied by command officers.

Celebrating seemed to begin the moment we set foot on the other side of the river. We drank from their never ending supply of vodka and never ending desire for us to drink more of it. The spontaneity and elation of this historic occasion resulted in our dancing with Russian women soldiers - another first. However, we also had to take cover when soldiers on horses fired their guns into the air from their prancing steeds.

This was truly a joyous and exuberant reunion. We traded medals, guns, indeed all kinds of memorabilia. It seemed that anything we had we traded without any thought about its value. We just wanted something we could take home and show other people. I still have a Russian cap with the Red Star which I proudly show as I relate these events.

Division Headquarters personnel saw me conversing with the Russians in my Polish language. Realizing I was fluent in that language, they quickly decided to fly me to Paris.

69th Inf. Div. Medical Doctor Arthur Seski (right) on his return from Paris after he spoke to the Russians on a Paris radio. Dr. Russman, the 69th Inf. Div. Dental Officer is on the left. (Photo provided by A. Seski)

Torgau banquet for high ranking officers of American and Russian armies. Gen. Reinhardt is on the left. (Photo provided by A. Seski)

Upon arrival, a Russian translator at the Seribe Hotel assisted me in both writing my speech and then in correcting my pronunciation of Russian words. As soon as my speech was ready, I was put on the Armed Forces Radio and my voice was beamed eastward for the Russians. Afterwards, I was given a tape and a plastic record of my talk which I still have. As soon as this assignment was completed I was flown back to 69th Division Headquarters in Germany.

With the collapse of the Third Reich, my next job was to help prepare our Division for the Asian Theater of War. This was rapidly accomplished and I was immediately transferred to the 9th Armored Division and given the same assignment with this Division. As soon as this repeat assignment was completed, I was again transferred to the 28th Division, fulfilling my same role as Division Surgeon. People often say the third time is a charm and so it was. After conducting the necessary medical requirements for stateside transfer, I was able to return with this Division to the United States.

Around 1980, I presented a paper in Moscow on Obstetrics and Gynecology. After the meeting, we were able to travel around in Russia with this medical group visiting a number of hospitals and obtaining an idea of how they were run. While traveling about, we were pleasantly surprised, especially at the artwork and beautiful buildings. The Russian people were all good-natured and we found that country's history very interesting.

1ST LT. WILLIAM LILIEN

Mr. Lilien passed away on November 7, 1992. However, his wife has kindly provided a picture and details for historical records and this book.

William Lilien was a First Lieutenant in G Company, 272nd Battalion of the 69th Infantry Division. On the way to Torgau in 1945, he was the leader of the very first platoon of Company G to enter Bad Ems and the city was surrendered to him. The Nazi Colonel in charge of the city presented his pistol to Lt. Lilien as an official act of surrender. Ordered not to cross the Elbe River, the Company went into a holding pattern. Troops began pouring back and forth over the Elbe on the 26th of April after patrol contacts had been made on the 25th.

Knowing that there were no more Germans between the two armies, celebrations were wildly enthusiastic, genuine and with a real show of comradeship. The Russian supply of vodka and the friendship on both sides seemed endless. It was a great disappointment to have Stalin start the "Cold War" soon after the soldiers on both sides had struggled so hard to achieve a victory which had molded a common bond.

Lt. Lilien always remembered the historic meeting in Torgau and rejoiced when the iron curtain came down. One of his wishes was to attend the 50th reunion.

The photograph shows Lt. Lilien on the left holding hands with a Russian soldier in front of the "East Meets West" sign erected on the banks of the Elbe River.

Lt. Lilian posing with a Russian soldier by the East Meets West sign on the outskirts of Torgau. (Photo provided by Lt. Lilian's wife)

THE SONGS OF WAR

by Robert M. Shaw
Rifleman, 273rd Regiment, Co. B.,
69th Infantry Division

"I surrender...!"

The cry behind me was loud and clear . . . my trigger finger flexed as I spun around . . . three yards point blank . . . Soldaten!

"Catch . . ." he screamed as he lobbed his rifle for me to catch. My first prisoner . . .God relaxed my finger ... we're alone in the forest I was scouting. His face was grey like his spotless wool trenchcoat. His boots gleamed. In perfect English: "Thank the Lord I'm your prisoner ... do you have a Chesterfield ... and what the hell are WE doing HERE at this time of OUR lives?"

We were but two thirty-second notes in the discordant symphony of war ... the power play of dollars and death. His name was Helmut ... it might have been Kurt or Wilhelm. To him I might have been Willy or Joe ... the naive teen-ager from ... "Leibergott! ... you are actually from New York City ... Carnegie Hall,

Accomplished musician Robert Shaw at one of the many pianos he played during combat. (Photo provided by R. M. Shaw)

Metropolitan Opera House, Radio City Music Hall ...?"

He whispered through the smoke of the Camel... "There I was in Chile, a lifetime away from the Third Reich... the favorite student of world-famous piano virtuoso Claudio Arrau. 'I teach you no more ... now return and use your musical talent to conquer your Fatherland'...And what of your conquest, Bob?"

How long did we speak of Bach, Glen Miller, Mozart, Pee Wee Russell, Chopin, Lauritz Melchior, Toscannini, Kirsten Flagstat, Arti Shaw ... it was "Play it again Sam" with a new script.

Too soon we shook hands firmly as only two pianists can, and the war was over for P.O.W. Helmut Kurt Wilhlem who could now see the long road to concert halls in Berlin, Frankfurt, London, Moscow and Chicago. For his captor, there were more tunes to play.

In Marburg, perhaps the startled sexton of Elizabethkirche still bores his grandchildren with the tale about this muddy Amerikanische soldaten who demanded and got the opportunity to improvise Baroque canons on the awesome cathedral's organ at two o'clock one rainy morning. But ... no doubt the loudest sound I made occurred when I caused Johann Sebastian Bach to roll over in his grave. After celebrating the liberation of Leipzig, I sobered up and set forth to the church of St. Thomas. Who did I encounter at the portal but Gunthur Ramin, Europe's leading organist. I pointed to his (Bach's) organloft, and wiggled my fingers as if to play a fugue. Was it with disbelief, reluctance, apprehension, or caution that he led me up the stairs to the keyboards? The church filled with my music.

Later that day I slept to dream that Ramin insisted that I replace him upon his retirement, "Wake up, private piano-player ... this is your platoon leader speaking..." Lt. Emil Guarino led me to an unscathed mansion in whose imposing ballroom was this massive Bluthner concert grand piano. Nervous servants scurried to set up chairs for several dozen U.S. Military Government staffers and German civilians. A tall, blond, pleasant gentleman approached and whispered into my ear: "I'm told that you will graciously accompany me for this impromptu concert honoring your comrades who have liberated our fair city...I am August Seider, Heldentenor of Leipzig, Please ..." He gestured to the music on the piano ...

How is mankind affected by the sounds and the music of war ... the discords of battle ... the silence of death ... the trumpeting of victory ... the dirges of funerals? The Heldentenor's heart was breaking as he sang to his picture-perfect wife and their beautiful children ... a fascinating story not to be revealed in this reminiscence.

And what of the broken hearts, bodies and minds of the countless Europeans and Americans who heard all the unforgettable sounds of war? Yet is there any meaningful music which does not have both bright and dark sounds? Is not the "plan of music" to harmonize and balance "all the sounds of Life" ?

After the Meeting on the Elbe at Torgau, these musical moments were shared with several compatible Soviet officers and soldiers. Each of them possessed the musical talent and background that could easily harmonize the ironic music of war. One Russian comrade, who studied music with Katchaturian and Shostakovich, offered this variation on the familiar phrase:

"Music can soothe not only the savage beast, but also the intellectual and political demons in all of us ... when our music plays an accompaniment for our March to a World of Harmony and Peace."

Robert Shaw in 1945 with a fellow 69th Inf. Div. soldier. (Photo provided by R. M. Shaw)

Robert Shaw leaning on a Sherman tank after the capture of Leipzig. (Photo provided by R. M. Shaw)

MY MOMENTS WITH THE RUSSIANS AT TORGAU

Based on information provided by Leo Gerger,
272nd Regiment, Hq. Co.,
69th Infantry Division

We had been waiting for the imminent link-up with the Russians, knowing it could take place any day or minute. I had my camera ready and felt fortunate to be able to be present the day of the meeting and for some days afterwards.

Our first proof that women were among the front line Russian fighting troops was their presence with these units. Many of these women were transportation controllers. I posed with one of them for a picture.

A barge system was constructed for crossing the Elbe River. As soon as it was operational, I snapped a picture of it carrying soldiers and an American jeep. The volume of people wanting to cross always exceeded the meager capacity. Good news travels fast and in one photo I took, a French officer can be seen on the barge as it is crossing the Elbe. He is on the left side of the photo with an American M.P. standing to his right. France sent officers and liaison personnel to this area to check on the POW/forced laborers and to screen for deserters.

Picture-taking by the East West sign was popular. Another of my photos shows a mixture of Russians and Americans posing by the big sign.

Indeed, these were euphoric days we had waited and fought for. Not everyone who had started out lived to see this historic moment, but we were grateful for their sacrifice that had helped make this day possible. Little did we suspect that

Stalin's picture on a train waiting to take Russian DPs and prisoners back to Russia. (Photo provided by L. Gerger)

Leo Gerger posing with a Russian transportation controller. (Photo provided by L. Gerger)

Stalin would soon block our new friendship. We now know that our soldier friends never bought that propaganda and now with the Berlin wall down, we celebrate with the same enthusiasm and esprit de corps as in April 1945, albeit a little slower. However, due to the passing years, we don't miss the abundance of vodka from those days.

Joint photograph of Russians and Americans posing by the East Meets West *sign. (Leo Gerger is in the middle.) (Photo provided by L. Gerger)*

French officer crossing on the barge. France sent officers and liason personnel to this area to check on the POW/forced laborers and to screen for deserters. (Photo provided by L. Gerger)

A barge pressed into service to move men and material across the Elbe River. (Photo provided by L. Gerger)

IMPRESSIONS

as told by John F. Pereira
T/Sgt., 271st Regiment, Co. A.,
69th Infantry Division

To have met the Russians under combat conditions, and knowing the background of the war, was an emotional experience. We knew there would be a meeting, but we didn't know when. I remember our orders when we attacked the Siegfried Line. "Gentlemen, we are breaking through the Siegfried racing across Germany and then linking up with the Russian army." When? We didn't know. Only when we arrived at the Mulde River did it seem possible.

What a wild bunch the Russians were! They even had women soldiers among the front line troops. If ever an army had cause to celebrate, theirs did. Emotions were indescribable. The link-up signaled the end of the war for us as well. It seemed each side tried to outdo the other releasing pent up emotions. AND the Russians had VODKA. When ever one bottle was empty, two more appeared. Drinking by combat troops must not have been a crime in Russia.

A multitude of emotions were wrapped up in the celebrating. No more cries of "Medic!" No more fire fights. The chance to go home and go home alive. And freedom for the German people from Nazi fascism, concentration camps, and firing squads if they dared to withdraw. Everyone had a right to celebrate. Everyone did.

John Pereira, wearing helmet, in 1945. (Photo provided by J. Pereira)

We were pulled back for occupation duties while awaiting further orders. Many of the 69th Infantry combat veterans were transferred to the 29th Infantry Division and sent to Bremmerhaven, Germany.

I became a First Sgt. and one of the pleasures of that job was to issue passes to Paris, Switzerland, and Copenhagen, Denmark. The general feeling of our troops was anti-German because of what Hitler had done to his people. There was sympathy for the Russians because they had been attacked by Hitler and had lost so many people in the war. Also, whenever we liberated POW's, the Russian soldiers were always the worst treated. Memories of the link-up are vague. My feeling today is that the Russians were misled by Stalin and some of his successors.

In retrospect, I feel justified in my participation in the war because I was serving my country to preserve our liberty and way of life. However, my thoughts for future generations are that they should work towards peace to prevent situations leading to conflicts such as World War II. This opinion is so strong for me that while showing my son-in-law my souvenir rifle recently, I was careful not to let my grandson see my German souvenirs. I didn't want him to have the impression and knowledge that his grandfather shot at other people. I believe we should seek peaceful solutions to our global problems.

John Pereira in 1994. (Photo by D. A. Philpott)

MEMORIES OF THE LINK-UP

as told by John S. Tounger,
271st Regiment, Co. D.,
69th Infantry Division

We were on patrol and made contact with the Russians in Torgau shortly after Robertson's patrol linked up with them. My first thought was, "Damn, I can't speak Russian!" But then neither could any of the other GI's. We immediately resorted to sign language. With the joy of our link-up and the desire to communicate, both sides did pretty well. The first thing I remember was the vast amount of vodka the Russians had. Judging by the volume, it must have been part of their rations because they kept producing it bottle after bottle. The taste of the vodka was really awful. I couldn't see how it could be Russian. In fact, I thought it tasted more like German V-2 juice.

Our jeep driver, Chuck Knebel (now deceased), took a picture of the Robertson patrol holding the homemade flag Robertson had made by busting into a drug-store and hastily using dyes to quickly mock-up something in order to signal the Russians it was Americans they were shooting at. The picture clearly shows a corner missing. We asked what had happened and were told that a Russian officer had torn off the corner as a souvenir of the historic meeting. Because there is at least one picture of this "flag" draped in such a way that this corner does not show, there is some doubt about the missing corner. However, Robertson verifies that indeed a corner was torn off the "flag." *(Ed. Note: This photo wasn't included because it is almost the same as Staub's.)*

Everyone who had a camera was taking pictures and we were no exception. I had my picture taken near a Russian artillery gun with a Russian soldier whom I assumed was in charge of it. His goggles and his pointing seemed to confirm that it was his artillery piece.

The third picture shows me returning from Torgau with a large number of German prisoners. This is what happened. On the way back, we encountered a German unit that was looking for a way to surrender. We had them place all their weapons in a big pile and then to form up so we could march them back to Eilenburg.

Russians using horse-drawn carts for transportation. This is a food wagon. (Photo by Chuck Knebel)

Several more Germans joined the march on the way. I remember thinking I had been on a number of patrols during the war, but this last one of the war for me was by far the most exciting and rewarding one. I could hardly sleep that night thinking about our 69th Infantry Division making the first contact with the Russians and the fact that the fighting should be over for us. I still regard it as one of the biggest moments of my life.

John Tounger posing with a Russian artillery soldier. (Photo by Chuck Knebel)

German Opal car (Olympia) used by Gen. Reinhardt for transportation in Europe. (Photo by Chuck Knebel)

Russian Artillery, 1945. (Photo by Chuck Knebel)

John Tounger after retirement. (Photo provided by J. Tounger)

A German wagon confiscated by the Russians. This was prohibited, but was permissible if it was used to chase Germans. (Photo by Chuck Knebel)

John Tounger returning to Eilenburg marching the approx. 100 German soldiers who surrendered to him. The line kept growing as he marched until he could no longer see the end of it. (Photo by Chuck Knebel)

FOUR COMMENTS

by Jim Stacy
Company Commander, 271st Regiment, Co. M.,
69th Infantry Division

1. As Company Commander, M Co., 271st Regiment, I can affirm that we had no indication of a link-up with the Russians; only that the forces were close to a meeting. My company was assigned as Flank Guards — to protect who or what was not defined — and only after the meeting of the senior officers of both armies did we learn of the occasion.

2. As a professional army officer, I regarded the Russians then as friendly Allies — the Germans as enemies.

3. My thought at the time of the link-up was, "Thank God. This will stop the killings, and my troops, as well as all other nationalities, can safely return home".

4. The youth of that period — some enlisted, some drafted — all worked toward a single goal; to end the war victoriously and return to their families and civilian life. May the youth of tomorrow, if called upon to serve, do so with a dedicated effort to match the youth of the 69th Infantry Division.

FIVE MINUTES BEFORE TWELVE, NEAR MÜLBERG OVER THE ELBE

by Henrich Zierdt
German Airforce Weather Assistant

18 April 1945. Russian armor was located in Neu-Petershain near Welzow. The orders to our airforce first read: Reinforce the SS-Units and hold the area just outside the airfield. Then we received orders to withdraw and march in the direction of the Elbe River. The commander of the eastern section of the front was General Schömer. He was well-known to me and generally disliked by everyone. Our Wehrmacht succeeded in withdrawing after the arrival of the Wafen-SS.

All of the officers and soldiers immediately realized that our fate was very uncertain. Consequently, there was a disintegration in command and we were suddenly without leadership. We resembled a scattered mass more than an organized army.

The Russians reached the front of the Welzow Airport on the evening of the 19th. Heavy fighting ensued and on the evening of the 20th, between 22:00 PM and 01:00 AM, the airfield and airport were in flames. Soldiers, civilians, and families fled in long wagon trains. Russian pilots straffed the fleeing columns so our scattered army traveled in the forest areas. I was part of a ten man group, three of whom had fought on the Russian Front. My job had been as a weather service assistant in the airforce. Our group decided not put up any resistance, but we were concerned since we did this on our own without knowing what the Hitler faithful would do. As we emerged from the wooded areas each evening, we saw destroyed equipment and many dead along the wagon trails.

We heard that the city of Welzow and the railway junction at Neu-Petershain had surrendered without a fight. Some of the men we encountered related that the Russians forced them to abandon their families, relinquishing their wives and women to them.

At sunrise on the 21st, we formed a group of about 200 men. Our goal was to reach the Elbe River. We didn't have a leader, but still had orders to stop the Russians on the Elbe River. As the Russian armor approached, the officers had deposited full packs of supplies in cars. We were told that a miracle weapon, the German built Messerschmidt 262, would be

Henry Zierdt during active duty as Luftwaffe Weather Assistant. (Photo provided by H. Zierdt)

Heinrich Zierdt at age 60 in 1972. (Photo provided by H. Zierdt)

used and with strong formations of SS, the Russians would be stopped. Our information about the location of the Russians came from mayors or Nazi departments. The fleeing columns increased daily. I spoke with two experienced soldiers who had escaped from the Russian front. Hitler supporters attempted to give us orders. However, I realized this pointless slaughter must end.

A Major tried to assume command of our group, stating that the Russians must be held at the Elbe River. Soon we heard sounds of Russian and German tanks. As I looked about the devastation, I only thought about my home and family. My wife was half buried when our home was bombed and became very mentally disturbed. My son had died at the age of 6 months. With the growing carnage, I thought only about ending this craziness. I still had my pistol. We had been warned not to give up to the Russians. By the evening of the 21st, the overflights by the Russian pilots ceased. Hundreds of men assembled at the Elbe River. They offered a lamentable picture, having endured much hardship to reach the Elbe. They had a last wish - to become American prisoners and they all wanted to cross the Mülberg or Torgau Bridges.

At the entrance to Mülberg was a hotel whose owners had left, but even before leaving, they had opened the hotel to anyone without charging. We entered it and with plenty of beer and wine available, celebrated as if we were victors. We celebrated the end of the Nazi reign and the passage out of the eastern front. I'm sure for many, this was their last night.

Late in the evening, four of us looked for a horse stall so we could sleep by the horses. A thunderstorm woke us early in the morning as the horses became restless. The storm was really a bombardment from the tanks. The Russians had reached Mülberg and were shelling the town. The hotel was emptied, but we were overlooked in the horse stall. We attempted to flee along houses and into the Elbe meadows. Civilians were also fleeing and large numbers people died from the shelling.

Soldiers from various units reached the Elbe and a Major gave the command: "The Elbe is to be defended and the Russian armor resisted!" The Russians attacked when the Germans resisted. They shelled everything that moved. Many of us felt that the war should end with this final battle. I saw many fall, including a Lieutenant Colonel who fell before me. I was trying to decide if I should shoot myself or if drowning would be best. I was trained as a life-guard - what should I do? Many of us jumped into the water to escape and were shot at by the Russians. In the final moments, I was pulled out by a fisherman and saved.

I could see Torgau in the distance. I was taken to a reserve military hospital in the Hotel Hubertusburg at Oschatz beyond the Elbe. Americans arrived before any German doctors appeared and we were transported by flat-bed trucks with stopovers at Prettin, Bad Schmiedeberg, and Bad Kreuznach-Bretzenheim. Then we were marched through the mud and wetness as rain and weather fronts had soaked the area. My uniform was wet.

It was the 27th and I was in Camp Bretzenheim. A steady stream of prisoners were arriving and the cramped conditions were dreadful. Many died while being held, especially those who had arrived with health problems. Some of the most common problems were scabies, dysentery, typhus, and heart and stomach ailments. We waited for death. Many became crazed and ran against the barbed wire attempting to escape or be shot in the process. The dead were taken to the graveyard on two-wheeled vegetable carts which were pushed and guided by two or three healthy war prisoners.

A subsequent letter of the German leader of the Bretzenheim group read:

"From April 1945 until September 1945, the number who died here was 22,000. Death seemed to be the only deliverance."

After 6 months without washing, shaving, being able to brush their teeth, or having clean uniforms, these soldiers were a pitiful sight. We wondered if the Russians would have treated us humanely and whether we would have let the Americans starve? Did they want to exterminate thousands of German soldiers? How much hatred was there against Nazi Germany? After all, millions of German citizens were anti-Hitler.

On the first of October, I was transported with a large group to a crowded prison camp at St. Antonio, France. We could see the Eifel Tower and knew we were near Paris. Here, we received medical attention. The ravages of war and close confinement took its toll and many died. At one point while I was in the hospital, I heard the voice of Jesus saying, "He who believes in me has eternal life". With my son dead, my wife insane, and my house demolished, I had little will to live. However, the doctors persevered and my health slowly improved.

In November, I was informed I would be released with the first group of moveable soldiers and injured invalids. Because my damaged home was in East Berlin, now occupied by the Russians, I was advised not to go there. My release read: further treatment to be given in Göttingen University Clinic. Without an apartment or work and still ill, I received hardship housing in Göttingen-Holtense.

THE LAST HOURS OF THE TORGAU FIRE BRIGADE

From The Recollections of Comrade Kitzig
by Hans Joachim Füssel

Since April 12, 1945, the Torgau People could hear cannon fire.

Pursuit pilots roared over the city shooting at anything that moved. The news about the heavy fighting at Eilenburg and Falkenberg created considerable unrest. The Torgau City Commander issued an evacuation order. Everyone had to leave the city until April 14th. There were red posters everywhere on the walls — Räumungsbefehl (i.e., evacuation orders). A ring around the bridgehead became armor-ditches and positions were dug along the Black ditch.

On the 15th of April, the Torgau Volkstrum received their assignment and moved out. The last troops available for the fight did not advance very far and were disarmed near the town of Gräfenhainichen. Going through Torgau's streets was agony because there was an unending flow of refugees coming over the Elbe bridge. All bridges in and outside the city were prepared for destruction.

Everywhere the City Burned

The last hours of the war demanded a most supreme sacrifice and a willingness to work from the men of the voluntary fire brigade in Torgau. Everywhere, it burned. On April 17, the siren of the city screamed. American pursuit pilots roared over the roofs. Bombs and bullets strafed whatever was at the railway station and the standing munition-trains which came from the nearby munition-factories at Süptitz, Elsnig and Mockrehna. Whole freight trains exploded with deafening noises throwing bazookas, grenades, bombs and ocean mines (for destroying ships) into the air.

Since 14:30 o'clock, the fire brigade men had been attempting for three hours, under these conditions, to prevent danger in the vicinity of these buildings and to keep objects away; a hopeless task. On the evening of the following day, the 18th of April, the administration buildings and the Braditzer stud farm burned after an air attack. Again Torgau's fire brigade men stood shoulder to shoulder with their neighbors in an attempt to fight the fire. Before the onset of night, the flames had to be extinguished. Previously undiscovered fires raged in the city on the 20th of April along the Repitzer path.

About 16 o'clock, the Allied bombers had set fire to the oil, airplane fuel storage tanks and loaded trains that were very high risk targets. The terrain of the Rhenania-Ossag-tank-camp and the area of the adjoining glasshouse resembled giant infernos. The blistering high energy material in the tank camp and in tank wagons on the rails of the camp and the neighboring glass factory caused enormous heat, continuous explosions and flames that could not be controlled.

From the area of the Torgau district, additional brigade men were ordered for support. As the fire brigade-men on the Repitzer path arrived, the asphalt in the street was burning. The men stood around with scant possibility to stop this inferno. The camp burned down entirely.

Under Peril of Their Own Life

The city had been confirmed a fortress and as of the 23rd of April, was under bombardment from Russian artillery pieces. There were four artillery pieces of a heavy flak battery in Torgau in the area of the former oil mill (fruits like poppy seed or rape were processed there) on Eilenburger Strasse which replied to the firing on the town. In an attempt to eliminate the Russian artillery pieces, they shot at them as well as other things. The Castle and Inn in Zwethau as well as the oldest building in Werdau was on fire. All of the construction burned to the ground. The defense of the city was a hopeless business and brought only new dangers. With the ongoing bombardment, the fire brigade-men on the 23 April, as of 16 o'clock, began working to extinguish the flames.

The first burned objects entered into the diary are the "Preussischer Hof" (i.e., a Prussian inn - restaurant and hotel), the church, the school gymnasium at school street, buildings on the Ritterstrasse, Fischerstrasse, and the coal dealer on Elbstrasse according to the last records of the fire brigade. Also residential barracks for foreign workers were hit and burned down. Hartenfels Castle and the supply house suffered badly. While putting out the flames at the storage place of the coal trader, a machinist named Hugo Heinrich was standing beside his pump on the Elbe when he received a bullet through his helmet which gave him a head wound. Fortunately, the wound was not severe.

On the same day at the town hall, there were dead people. While the Americans continued to bombard Eilenburg, a group of fire brigade men from Torgau disregarded their own safety to build a small dam with the only vehicle that they possessed, to help the suffering population of the blistering city. Comrades Karrass and Winzer were wounded during the bombardment. Their fire fighting vehicle was heavily damaged and had to be drawn back to Torgau by horses.

The City Becomes the Fighting Place

of the Russian Takeover

On April 25, we read in the participation diary that at 02:15 o'clock; "evacuation-command received at 2:15 AM. City is handed over to the Russians without fighting: Retreat to the southwest part of the district, Richter". On the morning of the same day towards 03:30 o'clock, powerful detonations startled the people. The railroad and the street-bridges over the Elbe and a number of smaller bridges through and in front of the city were exploded on a command from German soldiers. The evacuation-command was regarded as also applying to the fire brigade-men on April 25, 1945, as Friedrich Kitzig remembers. Most of the fire brigade people went in the direction of Eilenburg. Only a few remained with the firemen's apparatus in the fire house.

In front of Eilenburg, we separated. I traveled with those who wanted to go to Bad Düben. In Pristäblich, I turned off to the right in the direction of Torgau. I had the pointless feeling about failing to have enough food and drink. We were located between Americans and Russians and civilians escaping amid a helpless mass and soldiers. Often pursuit pilots flew over us thundering away. We were in constant danger exposed to their bombardment.

Worse, we could not look after our homes. Above Pressel Weidenhai rode back with my bicycle on the shortest path and arrived here near noon April 26. In Torgau, I met Russian and American soldiers, who were patrolling streets arm in arm.

At the market place, I found one of our fire brigade-pumps with all the acces ries beside the cistern. The equipment was abandoned. I gathered three help and brought the pump into position. With citizens Münster, Liebisch and Keil, returned the fire fighting apparatus to the building near the Prussian Inn aga The large building in the Bäckerstrasse burned brightly. The water in the cist under the marketplace was soon spent. A different place to obtain water for fighting was found in the Palace yard unloading pond. We laboriously dragged pump, hoses and all the implements to that area. With the equipment again ope tional, we took the hoses from the castle over to the Ritterstrasse where the fire returned to life. First came darkness and closing time which forced us to m adjustments for the extinguishing work. When I came to work the next morn the fire engine, hoses and all the appliances were missing."

Most of this information has come from the recollections of Comrade Kitzig.

FIRST TORGAU MAYOR APPOINTED BY U.S. COMMANDER

The first mayor was the fire brigade-leader
by Hans Joachim Füssel

On April 27, the leader of the voluntary fire brigade and savings bank secretary, Otto Richter, became commissioner mayor of Torgau, appointed by the American Commander. The Russian Commander authenticated this decision two days later. According to the employment records, Richter remained mayor until May 29, 1945. He was followed in this function by the anti-fascist Max Listing. Richter had been a member of the Nazi-party and therefore he was replaced, according to the declarations of the veterans.

The relationship between the Soviet Commander and the Torgau fire brigade was constructive from the beginning. The Commander posted a notice at the door of the fire station stating that soldiers and civilians were forbidden to enter the building. Four head fire brigade-men were employed under his direction. He investigated employment qualifications personally and provided the necessary fuel for the fire truck and pumps. The Torgauer fire brigade was under the personal protection of the city-commaders.

The first meeting of Torgau citizens took place a few days after the occupation by the Red Army on order of the Russian Commander at the sporting grounds beside the fire-station. The City Commander demanded from the inhabitants of Torgau calmness and quietness and promised help and work. The first efforts were aimed at the reconstruction of the shattered Elbe-bridges, the bridge over the Red Furth, the railroad yard and railroad routes.

1985 Link-up Celebration in Torgau, Germany. (Photo provided by the Torgau Kulturhaus)

1991 Elbe Days in Torgau, Germany. (Photo provided by the Torgau Kulturhaus)

THE "DOWN BY THE RIVERSIDE" STORY

The origin and development of an idea for the people
of the world to better understand each other.

by Günter Schöne,
Editor of the German version
of Hands Across The Elbe

Since the political change in East Germany, there has been an international celebration at the Elbe River in Torgau of April 25th, the day of the Link-up and of understanding among nations. We had this festivity for the 5th time on April 25, 1994. When I, as one of the founders of this annual event, think about its history, there are some personal points which eventually led to what is now known as the international "Down By The Riverside" celebration. Reporters often ask me about the starting point for such an event. Perhaps the following things are an answer.

My uncle, Erich Siptitz, was committed to exploring the history of Torgau. Even though he wrote books about it, this historical information was not what primarily interested me in the important events of April 25th. It was my childhood memories as well as this date which made a lasting impression on me.

Torgau was declared a fortress of the Nazis in 1945, when I was only 9 years old. My mother, grandmother, and I had only a hand cart when we left Torgau with other people to go to one of the neighboring villages. In our case, it was the village of Losswig where we arrived in the evening of April 14th. We stayed there with some relatives and I can clearly recall posters with evacuation orders hanging everywhere. I remember people with their hand carts leaving Torgau through the park and along the way to the riverport.

My father was taken to the so called Volksturm, which used elderly people as Hitler's last reserve of soldiers. His office in the district had to function up to the end of the war because they were trying to help people who had already been evacuated or bombed. When he became a Volksturm man he had to guard the so-called Panzersperren anti-tank barriers in the town. I remember my mother going there once in spite of the shooting from the eastern side and also going to our house again to fetch some necessary things.

The shelling of Torgau by the Russians from the far bank of the Elbe River was clearly seen from the house in Losswig where we stayed. Beyond the pastures and fields, the panorama of the city lay before me. From our viewpoint at Losswig, we later noticed the Americans coming down Dahlener Street. That must have been on April the 26th or 27th. Our semi-detached house in the western part of Torgau was occupied by them. To the east of "black creek" was the Russian sector where there were not only Russian soldiers but also Poles, former forced laborers, who could not go on to Poland because the Elbe Bridge had been blown up. Torgau was a divided town long before Berlin became one, if only for about 2 weeks.

At the end of April and beginning of May, my mother risked taking me with her to Torgau about 3 kilometers (2 miles) away. She wanted to know what had happened with our house. We had already known that Americans were in it. I was not allowed to go inside, but I saw everything from the window of a house opposite ours. There were a lot of wires and cables coming out. I also saw a picture of a young cousin of mine on the table of the sitting room and that the Americans even watered the rubber tree. The Americans who first occupied our house left behind a souvenir of a special kind which can still be noticed by the difference in colors on our sitting room door. Part of the door was damaged when it was forcefully opened and we can still see the split in it which was caused by the 69th Infantry Division. Of course at that time, I didn't know the name/number of the American Division.

The pleasure of being able to go back to our house after the Americans had left only lasted a short time. Obviously, our house must have been on a list of those recommended for lodging because the Russians soon took it over and we were forced to live in the neighboring house. After the Russians left, there were also Poles who came to German houses, including ours, and took everything they needed. Once they came with a horse-drawn wagon about 5:00AM and hammered violently on the door.

These were weeks when violence was quite normal and girls and women were raped. I remember clearly that my mother wore an old scarf so she didn't look as young as she was. Probably our house was one of the few where there were American and then Russian troops, so the Link-up has remained in my mind since my childhood. Another American "souvenir" which I found in my father's bookcase was a paper from a Baptist church in the southern United States. These were, of course, some impressions of my childhood, but later in the 50's and 60's I used to listen to RIAS radio. This was a radio in the American sector of Berlin and I recall that they spoke about a visit of Joe Polowsky in Torgau. I tape-recorded this message. In spite of the bad quality, this is still an interesting document after 35 years and it is a wonder to me that when I asked about it in 1990 at the RIAS archives, the people could not find it there.

As with most of the inhabitants of Torgau, I only heard about Polowsky being buried there after everything had already happened. The only thing I saw was some Americans from the Potsdam American U.S. Military Mission. Watching them triggered the return of my childhood impressions of seeing U.S. jeeps on their way to Berlin as they left Torgau. I remember the Americans distributing potato pancakes at that time. But in the 80's, 1985 for instance, there was a hard East-West confrontation and nobody thought about pancakes then because of the atomic race.

The 40th Anniversary of the Link-up was officially combined with a lot of propaganda. Never-the-less, some people of Torgau had a deep emotional contact with this former meeting on the banks of the Elbe River. Understanding each other like common people understand each other was something which this socialist unity party regime did not want to see, so they only took a few party members as contacts with the Americans. It seemed to be like contact with an enemy during the time of the East-West confrontation and common people were not allowed to talk to the American Veterans who had come to Torgau on that day.

American tourists were somewhat exotic in GDR everyday life. I know that GDR soldiers were not allowed to come home on leave in those days and others were only allowed to be there in civilian clothes. English teachers from the Torgau schools were not allowed to work as interpreters. Unfortunately, our guests did not seem to have noticed that there were only official people getting in contact with them. Most of the guests did not realize that they participated in a performance of sorts just to improve the image of the GDR states. The U. S. Government had officially resigned from taking part in Torgau. The reason was that three weeks before, one member of the U.S. Military Mission in Potsdam, Major Nicholson, had been shot in front of a Soviet military object near Ludwigslust. Instead of official U.S. participation, there were only some traveling groups and speeches by local leaders. However, we also heard of greetings by ex-presidents Nixon and Carter as well as Soviet Prime Minister Gorbachev.

A very interesting event for me was meeting Polowsky's son, Ted, who had separated himself from the official party and had wanted to see some Torgau sites completely privately. I succeeded in showing him the Castle Church in Hartenfels Castle as well as St. Mary's Church in town. I say succeeded because I was aware that we were observed by security people. When Ted Polowsky saw the guy behind me when we went down Ritter Street, I realized that it was the son-in-law of my garden neighbor who had to do his duty here. I think the American Veterans did not realize that the State Security (Stasi) of the GDR had organized the surveillance of them by other people in a military fashion. A special staff was responsible for these actions.

I myself became a prisoner for 4 hours in the cellars of the Torgau porcelain factory which is now a "Villeroy and Boch" factory again. When I had tried to take photos of the official reception in the Torgau Town Hall, I was not only banned from the building, but half an hour later was taken away from a snack bar on Torgau's Baker Street by policemen. I was allowed to eat my sausage, but then was taken to the Stasi. Even the two policemen who accompanied me were surprised that it took them such a long time to question me and to keep me there. I was only set free again when the official reception of the Veterans in Torgau had ended, so there was no longer any possibility of contact. Of course I walked to the Link-up Monument and saw some of the guests who were there for a farewell photo. I did not tell Ted Polowsky about what had happened to me because I did not want to disturb his impression of the festivities. Even Torgau's communist Mayor, Herr Strähle, had to notice later that the so called class enemy did not do anything serious against the GDR. They simply presented him with a Bible and Ted Polowsky held one in his arms to show it to the press photographers.

Because of my Polowsky contact, I was invited by LeRoy Wolins, the main sponsor for burying Joe Polowsky in Torgau in 1983, to see a film in Leipzig. The invitation was for the first performance of "An American Dreamer", a film about Joe Polowsky's life. The film was shown in a church and there were people of the so-called Torgau Seminar of the Christian Peace Conference present. I told those people about my phone call with the Polowsky Family which I had made at my own risk and without any official permission. The people of the Christian Peace Conference wanted to reimburse me for the cost of the telephone call, but the GDR Stasi must have thought differently about my actions. I noticed that on the following day when the members of the Christian Peace Conference were together in the Torgau Town Hall, I was not allowed to get in because I was neither a participant of the meeting nor a member of the Torgau Seminar group. Although I had been accepted the day before and had brought greetings of the Polowsky Family, my name was not on the official list. Even LeRoy Wolins' attempts to get me in were refused.

The idea of a first emotional East-West contact for common people must have settled in my mind. During an event of the International Dresden Dixieland Festival, I got an idea when the band was playing "Down by the Riverside". What about American and Russian military Dixieland bands marching from both sides of the

Elbe and meeting on the Elbe Bridge to the sounds of "Down by the Riverside"? This would symbolize the link-up at the historic Elbe Bridge in Torgau. This show would be followed by about 30 East German jazz bands marching through the town. At that time, it was of course not possible to think of European jazz bands taking part, not even West German ones being in Torgau. I wrote down my ideas later and about 1985, I thought that some official person might be interested in such a show. It was of course a mistake on my part to think that it would be possible to overcome barriers by contact as was done in 1945.

This obviously seemed to threaten the existence of the communist society which classified its population as common citizens and privileged ones who were allowed to travel to other countries. Practicing an oath of peace seemed to be something which only the state people and the secret security people were able to do.

What would have happened to an inhabitant of Torgau if he had acted like Joe Polowsky and tried to overcome the limits? I don't know if the American Elbe Veterans have thought about that. The former German Peace Council and especially one of its members named Frau Scheibe, who was working with everything involving the United States, thought that April 25th should not be anything of interest to the common man in the GDR. Only a very small group (I am speaking of the so-called Torgau Seminar of the Christian Peace Conference under the leadership of Professor Heinrich Fink) which could be supervised in their own Elbe Day activities were allowed to celebrate this historic event, but Professor Fink's demand to have a people's festival on that day was not allowed and disintegrated and so nothing came of it.

Torgau Bridge after being blown up in June 1994. (Photo by dpa; printed in June 18/19, 1994 Torgauer Allegemeine *newspaper)*

Nobody of the ruling party in those years thought that the idea of an April 25th festival was of any interest beyond their borders. That's why no personal or private initiatives were allowed and why the starting point for the "Down by the Riverside" project only came true some weeks after the political change in the GDR. I met a friend of mine, Dr. Uwe Niedersen, and told him of my idea to combine jazz and people's understanding with a peace symbol of the spiritual "Down by the Riverside", and I wanted to talk to the Mayor about all that. I asked him to come with me and he agreed. We were looking for at least a third man who sympathized with us, perhaps a Torgau clergyman who had already been active at the time of the political change. The mayor, the successor of the former Mayor, Herr Strähle, said we could start our citizen's initiative meeting at the Elbe. However, we soon realized that the political spring in eastern Europe had not been accepted in the minds of all the people yet.

The basic idea to have military Dixieland bands from the U.S.A. and the Soviet Union meeting on the Elbe Bridge, of course coming from the German missions, was threatened because the U.S.A. did not want to be together with the Soviets at a time when there were problems in the Baltic Republic of Lithuania. That's why we had a Russian military big band meeting a German big band for the link-up.

Never-the-less, together with American Veterans, it was a successful demonstration of what common people can do to demonstrate the idea of understanding among nations and of coming together. For the first time, Dixieland musicians of Germany, both East and West, were marching through the streets of Torgau together and demonstrating the idea of building bridges between nations. The year 1991 seemed to be a better one in the political sense. We had an agreement with a department of the U.S. Army in Berlin to take part in the symbolic show on the Elbe Bridge. Unfortunately, only a few hours before the buses were to depart from Berlin, we got a phone call saying that this was not possible. Who was to blame? The Ministry of Defense in Bonn or the Pentagon again? Nobody really knows, but we had organized a talk show, a concert in a church, and other things and our idea began to work.

The former German citizen's initiative resulted in the foundation of the Föderverein Europa Begegnungen, a society organizing meetings in Europe. In 1992, Dixieland musicians from East and West Europe met on the banks of the Elbe River and the U.S.A. agreed that their musicians would play together with Russians on Torgau's Elbe Bridge. Forty-seven years after the end of the war, we again saw American uniforms on Torgau's Elbe Bridge. The CBS report from that event was seen from Alaska to Hawaii and elsewhere. Prominent guests were, among others, Bill Robertson, Alexander Olshansky, and the Polowsky Family.

For the first time, reporters from military television AFNTV were allowed to enter the Soviet Garrison in Torgau. Unfortunately, politics again played a decisive role with the 4th "Down by the Riverside" Festival. We had no promise of American musicians taking part. Obviously the U.S.A. did not want to participate in anything which looked like a common farewell party with the Russians. The festival was enriched by a German Ukrainian forum organized by Dr. Niedersen. We also arranged an International Students' Conference. It was there where they signed a resolution to invite Bill Clinton to come and take part in the activities of the 50th Anniversary of both the Elbe Link-up and the foundation of the United Nations.

The invitations to Bill Clinton, to the Russian President, and to the General

LEIPZIGER VOLKSZEITUNG

4. JAHRGANG • Nr. 168   2 E 10181 A   MIT NACHRICHTEN FÜR BELGERN, DOMMITZSCH, SCHILDAU : DONNERSTAG, 21. JULI 1994

Streit um Sprengung der Elbbrücke bei Torgau – jetzt ein Thema fürs Oberlandesgericht

Die Torgauer Elbbrücke, von der bereits einige Teile weggesprengt wurden.
Foto: Wolfgang Sens

Bautzen (dpa/sn). Der Abriß der historischen Torgauer Elbbrücke hat ein gerichtliches Nachspiel. Das Sächsische Oberverwaltungsgericht will im nachhinein über die Rechtmäßigkeit des Abrisses entscheiden. Mit der Sprengung der Stahlbrücke, auf der sich in April 1945 amerikanische und sowjetische Soldaten trafen, seien zwar unverrückbare Umstände eingetreten, dennoch solle ein anhängiges Eilverfahren zu Ende gebracht werden, sagte eine Sprecherin des höchsten sächsischen Gerichts in Verwaltungsan- gelegenheiten gestern in Bautzen. Bereits nach Bekanntwerden der ersten, überraschenden Sprengung im Mai habe eine Privatperson Antrag auf eine einstweilige Verfügung gestellt. Das Oberverwaltungsgericht habe daraufhin den Antragsteller und das sächsische Wirtschaftsministerium als Antragsgegner um Stellungnahmen zu ihren Rechtsauffassungen zu dem Vorfall gebeten. Von beiden Seiten gebe es bislang keine Reaktionen. Der Antragsteller müsse jedoch mit einem Mißerfolg rechnen, hieß es.

Further destruction of the Torgau bridge. Photo by Wolfgang Sens; printed in July 1, 1994. "Leipziger Volkszeitung" newspaper.

Secretary of the United Nations proposes that their meeting should take place on the historic bridge of the first Link-up of East and West to reaffirm that the nations of the world came together for the first United Nations Conference. Musicians from all over the world would join in the peace appeal of "Down by the Riverside". Our group thinks such a demonstration of coming together and understanding each other is all the more necessary because the destruction of the historic Elbe Bridge indicates that some irresponsible politicians act without thinking about memorial places in Germany. Those who destroyed the historic bridge secretly without telling the people before they were going to do it need to hear the message of "Down by the Riverside" again.

In the German Bundestag, there is printed material numbered 12/94 in which is a demand for having a Glockenspiel in Torgau with the tune of the Torgau motto, "Down by the Riverside". Those people who secretly destroy memorial places should be disturbed by the sounds coming from Torgau. These sounds should foster their thinking.

Symbols Should Not Be Destroyed

The book cannot be completed without some remarks concerning what happened to the Torgau Elbe Bridge during the time "Hands Across The Elbe" was being prepared. Having become a symbol of peace and understanding for people during the decades after World War II, the overwhelming majority of people disagree with the way the Torgau bridge was destroyed by German transportation authorities. The secret destruction demonstrates their lack of historical responsibility. There was no moral justification for only these Germans to decide the fate of this place that symbolizes the Link-up between East and West and peace for all nations. Such a step was not their concern alone - it should have been considered by the European Community and the United States as well. Unfortunately, the voices of protest came too late, when the destruction had already started. Perhaps there was the common hope that some reasonable solution would be found in view of the 50th Anniversary of the Link-up. But the secret blowing up of the first part of the bridge in June and the later destruction revealed that this hope was in vain.

Readers of this book should at least get an impression of the historical significance of the Torgau Elbe bridge by the headlines in German and international newspapers:

"Nicht mehr lebendig Torgauer Elbbrücke wurde gesprengt"
No Longer Living - Torgau Bridge Destroyed
Sächsische Zeitun
June 18/19, 1994

"Torgauer Brücke blitzartig gesprengt"
Torgau Bridge Instantly Destroyed
Hannoversche Allgemeine Zeitung
June 18, 1994

"Brücke zur Geschichte abegebrochen In Torgau wurde mehr demonstriert als nur die Sprengkraft dumm-deutscher Ignoranz"
Bridge of History Broken In Torgau there was a demonstration of dumb German ignorance
Neues Deutschland
June 18/19, 1994

"Aus für ein Stück Geschichte: Torgauer Brücke heimlich gesprengt"
A piece of history: Torgau Bridge secretly destroyed
Leipziger Volkszeitung
June 18, 1994

"Streit um Sprengung der Elbbrücke bei Torgaujetzt ein Thema fürs Oberlandesgericht"
Dispute about the destruction of the Elbe Bridge at Torgau - now a theme for the regional court of appeal
Leipziger Volkszeitung
July 21, 1994

"Germans destroy historic bridge"
The *TIMES* Saturday European News
June 18, 1994.

(Günter Schöne, editor of the German version)

LILACS, MEETINGS, AND OATHS— MEMORIES OF RUSSIAN AND UKRAINIAN WORLD WAR II VETERANS

The editors used information provided by A. Olshansky and A. Silvashko to create a comprehensive narrative which we believe captures the essence of the original material. The Russian translation from newspaper and magazine articles and other documents was done primarily by M. Bukhankova. The names of individual authors of articles and information about them is provided at the end of this text.

ALEXANDER OLSHANSKY begins:

Looking at the map of Germany, one can see the names of many big cities situated at the borders of the Elbe River. Cities like Magdeburg, Hamburg, and many small towns. Two of these are Torgau and Strehla. It was between these two cities in the center of Germany that there was a meeting between the Soviet and American soldiers on the banks of the Elbe River on April 25, 1945.

Russian newspapers reported that troops of their 58th Guards Division met scouts from the American 69th Infantry Division in the area of Strehla at the Elbe River at 13:30. At 15:30 on the same day, on the banks of the Elbe in the area of Torgau, the battalion of the 173rd Regiment from the same 58th Guards Division met with another patrol of the 69th Infantry Division.

The expression "Meeting at the Elbe" is now part of the history of the Second World War. It remains as a symbol of the handshakes of the Allied military companions against Hitler's Germany.

At the very same day - at the other end of the globe - in San Francisco, was the opening session which founded the United Nations Organization. "We believed in its capability to make happen the will to peace and the friendship of our people and their sons who gave each other hugs at the borders of the Elbe."

The following is from an account by LEONID VOLODARSKY about meetings with Major Craig's patrols:

Unfortunately, there is no information in contemporary literature about some events regarding our meeting with the American reconnaissance patrol group. Special scouts in the patrol groups of Major Craig's American soldiers arrived at the crossing at the village of Kreinitz.

We were told that the headquarters of his regiment (in Wurzen) was in trouble because they didn't have any information about the special reconnaissance patrol group of Lieutenant Kotzebue. They were looking for the patrol groups by plane, but found nothing, so the decision was made to send someone to the area of the city of Strehla.

At 15:00, a group from the regiment placement met two jeeps which had been sent by Lieutenant Kotzebue to the headquarters of the regiment.

After exchanging information, Major Craig's group, with the permission of their commanders, proceeded to the Elbe River using seven jeeps. Not knowing Lieutenant Kotzebue's exact route, they followed a slightly distorted one. At the village of

Gen. Olshansky (left) and "Buck" Kotzebue (right) at the Elbe River in 1985. (Photo provided by A. Olshansky)

Gen. Alexander Olshansky— Torgau, Germany, April 25, 1994. (Photo provided by Torgau Kulturhaus)

Lekvitz, Major Craig's group met a Russian cavalry regiment. There were about 20 horse-riders and one motorcyclist. After a brief exchange of greetings and taking pictures, they went towards the Elbe in the direction of Strehla. They arrived there about 16:00. With the help of a citizen in the main square, they tried to find out the location of the Russian troop's office. But, at this time, there weren't any official Russian troops in Strehla. After briefly stopping cars in the main street of the city, they went to the Elbe River where they met the Russian soldiers. These troops explained to Major Craig and his soldiers about the special reconnaissance patrol group of Lieutenant Kotzebue that had crossed the Elbe River at the village of Kreinitz. Major Craig's group went to Kreinitz and crossed the Elbe with the same ferry.

In our (i.e., the Russian) and different foreign literature, we have a different picture of the meeting of the Russian cavalry and Major Craig's soldiers. The Russian cavalry group was completing the same task as Lieutenant Goloborodko's reconnaissance group. But the cavalry didn't know anything about the identification system of the signals and they couldn't verify any coordinates of their meeting.

The memory of that time is that they thought it was a special scouting reconnaissance regiment of the 1st Cavalry Guards Regiment. In the documents, information was found about the action taken by the 1st Cavalry Regiment of General-Lieutenant Barabanov and we knew that this course took a great deal of effort to move forward to the Elbe. In the picture, we can see the cavalry in special uniforms with sabers, looking very brave. They are standing on the ground beside their horses. We can see on these pictures officers of the American army too. On the second picture, the cavalrymen are staying very close to the Elbe. The group of Goloborodko was dressed in a very different way. Some were wearing special winter hats and others, field caps. All the Americans were wearing helmets and on their helmets were camouflage nets. In Kotzebue's group, big white stars were on the helmets and on the hoods of the jeeps. The American soldiers from Craig's patrol and Robertson's soldiers didn't have any marking signs on their helmets or the hoods of the jeeps. (Ed. note: The photos described above were not in the material which was sent to us.)

When Robertson entered Torgau, he didn't even have green rockets. The meeting at Torgau happened very suddenly and spontaneously. From the town of Strehla, we took the American patrol to the village of Kreinitz and at the same time in Torgau,

Americans took assistant commander of the 173rd Regiment, Lieutenant Colonel Larionov, combat Captain Nyeda, platoon commander Lieutenant Silvashko, and Sergeant Andreyev. Robertson could do that only because he didn't tell Larionov that the Division was located in the city of Wurtzen at the Mulde River. At the meeting in Kreinitz, Lieutenant Kotzebue and Major Craig told us and showed us on the map that a patrol for observation of the Elbe would be sent from the town of Wurtzen and also Eilenburg, Trebsen, and different directions.

Some soldiers of Major Craig's group had cameras and took many pictures. It seemed to me that their scouts not only had personal cameras, but also movie-cameras. Probably, they had to confirm the information they got not only orally and in writing, but also with pictures. They took pictures not only of this meeting, but the ferry in the vicinity of Strehla, the low temporary bridge, and some other objects.

At the meeting in Kreinitz, Major Craig said - probably he was just kidding or maybe he was serious - it was hard to understand this at those times - that the radio station of Lieutenant Kotzebue was working well, but he was so agitated that he incorrectly tuned in and confused one wavelength with another. So people were laughing and kidding. We didn't have any qualified translator during the meeting. Igor Belousovich was used as a translator. In Craig's group and in Lieutenant Kotzebue's patrol were some soldiers who could understand German and who could, with some difficulty, talk with us. Polowsky was one of them. It seems to me he could speak Polish and German. Many of them talked with our translator, Captain Kogan, in German.

The exchange of souvenirs was so intense that at times we didn't even have buttons on our shirts. We exchanged watches, emblems, symbols, etc.

The meeting at the Elbe was the meeting of two very friendly armies who fought fascism in Germany and the big cause of protecting the peace and safety of all the people on earth.

GREGORI GOLOBORODKO, a Lieutenant of the Soviet Army at that time, gave this account:

Early in the morning of April 25th, the company which I commanded was going across the Elbe in the exact place where Hitler's troops had just blown up 3 bridges. On the west side of the Elbe was the small town of Strehla, to the south of Torgau.

The observation point of the commander of the 175th Regiment was located on top of the bell tower of the church in the village of Kreinitz on the east side of the Elbe. The fog densely blanketed the river and the meadow. We moved out to the dam along the river to a ridge northwest of Strehla and entrenched ourselves. The sun rose. The fog disappeared, but the city showed no sign of life. It was as if it was dead.

(L to R): Bill Robertson, Gen. Alexander Olshansky and Gen. Vladimir Orlov in 1992 in Torgau, Germany. (Photo provided by E. Bräunlich)

A little later, our scout told us that the small town was occupied by the Americans. The German front was finally crossed from East to West and we didn't have the enemy in front of us. We heard the noise of cars from the town.

A special red rocket flew in the air from our side. In response, we saw a green one in the suburb of the town and at the same time, we saw many American soldiers who were hidden before. This very noisy crowd was running toward us. We heard very distantly the greeting, "Russia-America", "America-Russia".

Their commander came to me and we had a firm handshake. It was Lieutenant Buck Kotzebue. And it was the first meeting of the soldiers of the united armies. After that was a dinner in the village of Kreinitz and the official meeting of the commanders of the Regiment and Division. And here is the story of the American Army sergeant, Joe Polowsky:

- At dawn, our patrol went from our position about 25 miles from the Mulde River and our task was to get in touch with the troops of the Soviet Army. After going through no-man's-land, our Infantry soldiers reached the west side of the Elbe at 10:30 in the morning of April 25, 1945. But around us, we saw the remains of Hitler's troops who were in front of us. Suddenly, we saw a special red rocket. We responded with green rockets and when we got to the edge, we saw the Soviet troops.

The waves of the Elbe were very fast because of the spring rain. The only thing which could help us and which was in our disposition to get to the other side was a small wooden boat attached with a lock. We took this boat. (Ed. note: The lock was reportedly blown off by means of a hand grenade, but it was probably shot off.) The water was flowing very fast, but we finally got to the east side.

The American Infantry crossed the Elbe with sentiments of joy and relief. They were sure of their future and they were hugged by the soldiers of the armies of Marshals Zhukov and Konev who marched from the Volga to the Elbe. This meeting took place at noon on the 25th of April, 1945.

———————

An article by GREGORY PROKOPYEV about the historic meeting provides the following details:

The meeting with allied troops was especially noticed by an order of the Supreme Commander-In-Chief. In honor of this historic event, a special salute was given on April 27th in the Soviet capital of Russia; Moscow. As a tribute to the valiant troops of the 1st Ukrainian Front and our Anglo-American troops, 324 artillary guns fired a 24 gun-salute.

- - -

Soviet troops under the command of Lieutenant General Alexei S. Zhadov and the troops of the first American Army under the command of Lieutenant General Courtney Hodges divided the front of the fascist troops. The result was brilliant and enemy troops located in the north and in the south of Germany were separated from each other.

Exactly the same day - April 25 - Berlin was surrounded by the troops of Soviet Marshals G. K. Zhukov and I. S. Konev.

The meeting at the Elbe was celebrated with joy and happiness. From the boat on our side, we saw the commander of the 69th Infantry American Division, Major General Reinhardt, with a big group of officers and soldiers. We saw the national flags of three nations. The commander of our 58th Guard Division, Major General A. V. Rusakov, went to meet the Americans at the river.

The handshakes and friendly hugs began. Standing there, embracing each other, were Nikolai Andrev from Kurst and Frank Huff from Virginia, Peter Ugnatev from Dniepropetrovsk and James McDonnell from Massachusetts, Nikoli Volkov from Bashkir and William Robertson from Los Angeles.

Soviet soldiers sang their most loved songs and the Americans helped them. Souvenirs were exchanged.

The meeting of the generals and their officers and soldiers continued at the tables which were served very simply. Photocorrespondents and film makers, ours and from the other side of the Elbe, took pictures about the first handshake of Soviet and American soldiers. Correspondents wrote their material there.

Friendly meetings very much like this took place at many locations at the west and east, from the city of Torgau to the city of Muhlburg. Over there, it was very still, but at the north and south, the artillery was working. In the sky, we saw planes attacking planes and we remembered the tanks and Infantry. In Berlin, the Soviet Army was breaking the enemy's defense step by step.

Many soldiers and officers who went from the Volga and the Don to the Elbe were awarded American orders and medals. Many American soldiers and officers from the 69th Infantry Division were awarded Soviet orders.

During the friendly talks with the American soldiers and officers, we felt that they didn't know what the war really meant. In America, houses weren't burned. Children didn't cry over their dead mothers. Americans didn't see our destroyed cities and countries. They didn't know that in this war, we lost about 20 million Soviet people.

ALEXANDER GORDEYEV describes the meeting and the birth of the Spirit of the Elbe this way:

On April 23rd, the 175th Regiment was at the Elbe in the area of the village of Kreinitz and was moving toward the city of Strehla.

I gave instructions to the commander of the 6th Company of the 2nd Battalion, First Lieutenant Goloborodko, to prepare a group of people to take some action on the western bank of the Elbe. We gathered the boats and other things. An order issued by the commander of the 5th Guards Army, Colonel General Zhadov, said: "The task is to take a crossing place at the Elbe River and hold it, especially if there are no allied troops".

The crossing of the patrol to the west bank was supposed to be in the morning of April 25th. We knew that the crossing place at the Elbe was more than 150 meters wide. The speed of the flow was very high - more than 1 meter in 1 second. All measures were taken the way we did during the crossing of such rivers as the Dnieper, the Dnester, the Vistula, and the Oder.

In the evening of April 24th, I personally made the task more precise on that very deep and very wide reconnaissance of the enemy in the area of the future attack, including behind the Elbe where the American troops were supposed to be. So it was possible to meet them. In this case, the signal was from our side - the red rocket - and from the American side - the green one.

We crossed the river early in the morning in the fog using a ferry cable. We were moving to the south in the direction of Strehla. Not far from the town, we saw a ridge and entrenched ourselves. After several hours of observation, we didn't get any results. The town and the road were still and deserted. We sent several people to the closest home to investigate the situation.

Approximately mid-day, we heard the noise of machines. Several minutes after that, we saw our people running to us and screaming. We thought that the enemy was in the town and got ready to fight. At the same time, in the area of the town, we saw a green rocket. In response, First Lieutenant G. Goloborodko shot a red one. At this moment, from the houses, we saw soldiers running and screaming, "Russia-America", "America-Russia". The extremely intense waiting for the attack was suddenly changed by the joy of the meeting.

Col. Charles Adams, Commander of the US 273d Regt., leads American/Soviet soldiers in victory toast at regimental headquarters at Trebsen. From left: Lt. Alexander Silvashko, Maj. Anafim Larionov, Col. Adams, Sgt. Nikolai Andreyev (whom Robertson first met on the Torgau roadbridge) and Robertson. (Text quoted from Yanks Meet Reds; photo provided by M. Scott. Source: Bill Robertson)

The cheers and congratulations began. We explained ourselves using sign-language. With the noise, it was hard to understand anything. We found out that it was the American patrol with Lieutenant Albert Kotzebue and more than twenty soldiers with six "jeeps". First Lieutenant Goloborodko exchanged information with Lieutenant Kotzebue about the situation of their troops and then made a report to his commander about the meeting with the American patrol and was given directions to invite Kotzebue with his soldiers to Kreinitz at the right bank of the Elbe. The Americans made a raft with a rubber inflatable boat and used the

Russian pontoon bridge erected below destroyed Torgau bridge. (Photo by Charles Weaver of Columbus, OH)

rest of the German ferry crossing to ferry to our side. Military nurse, L. Kozenchenko, presented the American soldiers with a bouquet of April lilacs.

In Kreinitz, by this time, preparations were made for the meeting. My assistants, Lieutenant-Colonels Y. Kozlov and T. Bitarov, the Chief of Staff of the Division, Lieutenant Colonel S. Rudnik, Chief of Staff of Artillery, Major A. Ivanov, and Assistant Chief of Staff of the Political Division by the Young Communist League, Captain V. Orlov, arrived at the ferry-crossing.

The meeting in Kreinitz was opened by Lieutenant Kotzebue's announcement introducing the soldiers of his reconnaissance patrol. He reported to the 175th Guards Infantry Regiment commander, but in English. After that, the guests were invited to dinner. At the beginning, there were speeches, discussions, showing pictures to each other, and examinations of the American and Soviet medals. They made themselves understood with gestures, smiles, and friendly slaps. The guests understood well the words "Stalingrad, Moscow, Volga, Oder, Vistula, Don, and Warsaw". Photocorrespondant for the newspaper "Pravda", Alexander Ustinov, arrived by plane. He took some pictures of the first part of the meeting and immediately was taken to Moscow. Later, correspondents S. A. Krivisky and others arrived.

On the same day, a few hours later, 40km downstream by the Elbe, in the vicinity of the city of Torgau on the right flank of our Division, a second meeting was going on. Soldiers of the sub-machine gun platoon led by Lieutenant Alexander Silvashko from the 173rd Guards Infantry Regiment met the American patrol consisting of Second Lieutenant William D. Robertson and privates Frank A. Huff, Paul Staub and James McDonnell.

The celebration and happiness was passed on following the meeting of the allied troops at the Elbe. Soldiers and officers of the allied armies firmly embraced and gave each other souvenirs. Many of our officers cut off the buttons from their overcoats and shirts - they gave them as remembrances. The American soldiers highly regarded the symbols, rank stripes, orders and medals of our Guards. They showed pictures of wives and children, took photographs, and exchanged autographs.

The Soviet and American soldiers, in the meeting on the bank of the Elbe, took an oath to preserve and strengthen the spirit of the Elbe, the spirit of friendship and mutual understanding between our nations. The meeting at the Elbe was the meeting of two armies, fighting against a common enemy - fascist Germany. We, the Soviet veterans of the meeting at the Elbe, remain loyal to the mutual oath - to strengthen peace on earth. We are loyal to these memories and are glad when the testimony reaches us that there are a lot of people in the United States who feel the same.

A. Olshansky provided the following information:
Ten years later, in 1955, Moscow accepted a group of Americans who had been participants in the meeting at the Elbe. They were invited by the Soviet veterans.

It was the month of May. It was spring. The sun was shining. But it was the time of the "Cold War". The plane on which the nine American soldiers from that distant time were flying was just like the first swallows flying after a cold winter - the symbol of a new relationship between the former allies.

The desire of our nations to return to the "Spirit of the Elbe" was without any doubt. In the U.S.A., an organization of American participants sprang up in memory of this meeting. In an open letter, they invited the Soviet veterans to come to Washington on April 25th to celebrate the 10th Anniversary. The Soviet side accepted this offer with joy, but (and WHY, it could not be said) somebody in the U.S.A. (I understand it wasn't the veterans) arranged the arrival of our delegation in a way that it couldn't take place. Then the Soviet veterans invited their American colleagues without any conditions. (Ed. Note: In the Yanks Meet Reds chapter "Murry Schulman", it says that when the Russians made their application to come to the United States, they were told they had to be fingerprinted. Apparently, only criminals were fingerprinted in Russia, so the Soviet veterans refused to be fingerprinted. Instead, they invited the Americans to come to Russia.)

And so the veterans of the Elbe from the U.S.A. were in Moscow. The leader of the group was Joseph Polowsky - the former sergeant from Lieutenant Buck Kotzebue's patrol. At the meeting with him was textile worker Charles Forrester, engineer William Wells, farmer Elijah Sams, businessmen Robert Haag, Murry Shulman, Claude Moore, and office workers Fred Johnston and Bill Shiver. (Ed. Note: In the Yanks Meet Reds chapter "Murry Schulman", Edwin Jeary is listed instead of William Wells.)

The American veterans visited Soviet territory for 4 days. Where did they go and what did they see - these nine American soldiers from the Second War who flew to Moscow to celebrate the 10th Anniversary of the common victory with us?

First of all - they got to know the Soviet capital, the architectural monuments, and the many newly constructed works. Here the Mount of Lenin is a place from which there is a good view of the silvery ribbon of the Moscow River surrounding the city. Red Square, with the old tower of the Kremlin, with the Mausoleum of the founder of the Soviet State, Vladimir Lenin... Many new buildings decorated with festive flags fluttering in the spring breeze, many vast squares and streets... "A big city in a big country", said Joseph Polowsky as he looked from the Mount of Lenin over the panorama of the city of Moscow.

In the central home of the Soviet Army, the guests were met by a group of Soviet veterans including Gregori Goloborodko. A former First Lieutenant, he was working then as an assembly mechanical engineer at one of the collective farms in the Poltava area of the Ukraine. There were many hugs and firm handshakes at the meetings...

A nice surprise for the American guests was the picture exhibition of those distant events in April 1945.

With emotion and joy and with surprise, they recognized themselves and their friends in Alexander Ustinov's pictures:

- Oh, look, this is Polowsky...how eloquent he looks!... "Joseph, is it possible this is your younger brother?", asked one American. - And here is Shiver!... Look, it really is Shiver!... This exhibition must be shown in the States!

The people were so touched that they had tears in their eyes. They were suddenly closer to the past and saw the war like it really was at the time and they knew each other. Here is Sergeant Rodinov. Where is he now? He is a teacher in an orphanage. Here is Private V. Korchagin. And what has he become in ten years? He completed Leningrad University. Here is Sergeant A. Baranov. What was his destiny? He is an engineer at a Moscow factory...

Questions and addresses were exchanged. The American and Russian participants of the meeting at the Elbe were touched by the feelings that emerged and promised each other to be faithful to their precious friendship.

After this meeting, an emotional conversation started a meeting later. Joseph Polowsky said:

- We cannot forget that ten years ago, we and the Russians met as friends. Conscience and memory prompts us: both of our countries came to the conclusion that it is proper for Americans and Russians to meet again as friends. Let the resolution that we had at the Elbe not be abandoned to this day. We should unite our efforts to fulfill the oath said at the Elbe.

In response, Alexander Silvashko, former Lieutenant and then the director of a school in Byelorussia said:

- Millions of people died and that's why we cannot be resigned to the renaissance of reactionary forces and war. Let our meeting make a normal relationship between our countries in the interest of peace for the whole world. It doesn't matter that we speak different languages. We understand each other, here in Moscow, like we understood each other at the Elbe. We were good soldiers and now we will fight for peace on the whole planet. Yes the friendship between the American and Soviet people is thriving!

The words of the veterans made a big impression on those who were in the hall at that time. Nobody was shy about their feelings. Farmer Elijah Sams from North Carolina was wiping his tears. When a soldier cries, people should think about it. The most important thing is that victory earned with blood not be taken away. He fought for peace and wants peace.

The American veterans had a good time. Some of them went to a collective farm near Moscow. They visited a rural school and went to the class during the lesson. Somebody asked: "Which of you children had fathers or brothers who participated in the war?" And suddenly, the whole class raised their hands. The Americans winced. Elijah Sams wrote a comment in the school's book next to the name of their group: "I hope that the children I saw here and my children will not participate in a war like the past one that we Russian and American veterans were in."

Another group of guests visited the production of the newspaper, "Pravda", where the veterans met with political reviewer, Uri Zhukov, and other journalists. Then all nine Americans, together with the Soviet veterans, visited the Kremlin. They walked around the city with the crowds in the street. They were with the marshal of the Soviet Union, V. Sokolovsky, at a reception held in their honor.

The Spirit of the Elbe is sacred. We will not forget.

LEONID VOLODARSKY comments on the 10th and 20th Anniversary meetings:
American veterans J. Polowsky, C. Moore, F. Johnston, W. Wells, R. Haag, M. Schulman, B. Shiver, C. Forrester, and E. Sams were at the 10th Anniversary meeting of the allied troops at the Elbe which was celebrated in Moscow during May of 1955. They met Soviet veterans G. Goloborodko, A. Silvashko, A. Baranov, V. Korchagi, E. Samchuck, and P. Alexev.

The first meeting of the allied troops at the Elbe was followed by the capitulation of fascist Germany and the end of the war in Europe. At the second meeting of American and Soviet veterans in Moscow, after 10 years, the "Cold War" has become "warmer".

- - -

During the 20th Anniversary of the victory over fascist Germany, Soviet veterans confirmed their loyalty to the oath which was given during the historic meeting with the American soldiers at the Elbe not to allow the flames of war to once again flare up in the world.

Former technical Sergeant A. M. Baranov, Lieutenant Colonel A. V. Olshansky, and retired Colonel E. E. Samchuck, during a press-conference in the Government Committee of the Soviet Minister of the U.S.S.R., responding to the questions of Soviet and foreign correspondents on the cultural bond with foreign countries, reported they had not celebrated the Day of Victory over Hitler's Germany with their colleagues from the U.S.A. since they met in Moscow and in Washington. They said they were ready to continue their contacts with the American veterans about whom they continued to have good impressions.

An additional comment by Volodarsky: For the past 49 years, we Soviet veterans have remained loyal to our battle friendships and our mutual oath - to strengthen peace on earth together. We remember this oath and are glad when it reaches us that the American veterans remember it also.

The following material provided by A. Olshansky gives information about the 40th Anniversary activities and subsequent meetings of the veterans:

Preparations were made in many countries for the celebration of the 40th Anniversary of the victory over fascist Germany and the meeting of the Soviet and American soldiers at the Elbe. Television and movie studios of different countries in the world made movies about the war.

English television invited American veterans Albert Kotzebue and William Robertson and Soviet veterans Alexander Gordeyev, Alexander Silvashko, and Alexander Olshansky and photocorrespondent Alexander Ustinov and others for shooting films about the meeting at the Elbe. The shooting took place in Moscow, Minsk, Berlin and at the Elbe - in the cities of Torgau and Strehla. The filming took place prior to the third meeting of the veterans of the allied troops.

Alexander Olshansky recounts:

We arrived at the Elbe in March of 1985. With my help, we found the place of the former crossing in 1945. Our ferry, truthfully, was now motorized. The steel cable that formerly was used to pull across the Elbe, of course, was not there now. The old mooring was a thicket of grass. The waters of the Elbe had receded farther from the shore. One could see cobblestones protruding from the bottom of the shallow water near the moorings.

The movie producer for English television, Barry Cocroft, made it so that I got the news about the coming meeting with Albert only several minutes before the shooting began. Thanks to the "sudden action", he succeeded in capturing our truest feelings and emotions on film.

I was transported by ferry to the eastern shore, left there with some of the movie crew, and only after that was I told that A. Kotzebue would sail up to me from the west shore on the same ferry.

It is difficult to put into words what I felt when I knew that we would see each other in several minutes. A lot of things around us reminded me of what we had lived through 40 years ago. It was the same spring day with the sun peeping out. The village of Kreinitz, to the south of Torgau, was almost unchanged. But we ourselves had changed more. Was it only outwardly? On the ferry approaching the land was a medium height elderly man without a hat and with a pipe in his teeth. The pipe was most particularly important in the resemblance to the formerly young lieutenant from 1945. Would we recognize each other? Though it is true that we had pictures that were 40 years old, we hadn't met until this time. The ferry came closer and closer to everyone. By now, I could make out faces. Albert was wearing jeans and a lumberjacket. They reminded me of his former military uniform. The raft landed. At last I shook Albert's hand and said, "Hello, Buck! You haven't changed!" - "You haven't changed either!" he responded, and we embraced.

And right away he began to ask: "And where is Gregori Goloborodko and Gordeyev?"

"Goloborodko unfortunately died", I told him. "And you will see Gordeyev in Berlin and Torgau on April 25th. He is coming to the 40th Anniversary Celebration."

It took several days to shoot the movie. We had the evenings for talking and remembering. I had brought photographs taken by Alexander Ustinov of the meeting on the Elbe April 25, 1945, during the first moments of Albert's meeting with Gordeyev.

In those days, we didn't have other journalists at the Elbe. Albert hadn't seen these pictures, but he knew about the death of Joseph Polowsky. He also hadn't seen the pictures Ustinov put in the book, *Two Meetings,* which was edited after the 10th Anniversary of the meeting of the American and Soviet veterans in Moscow in 1955. Albert hadn't seen the 1955 pictures either.

Albert recognized everyone in these photographs and said: "This is textile worker Charles Forrester - he was recently at Joseph's funeral. It was very symbolic that Joseph was buried at the place of the former meeting. The solemn ceremony showed that the Chicago taxi driver's novel idea about mutual understanding and collaboration between the American and Soviet people is alive. He was able to get beyond national selfishness, rise above the contradicting policies and ideas and look beyond the basic differences. He knew it would be difficult to disregard one's personal interests. However, he understood their insignificance in comparison with the main values themselves - peace and a safe future. These exact values formed the main points vowed by the first soldiers at the Elbe, which the veterans repeatedly reaffirmed at their subsequent meetings."

"We were very grateful to Soviet veterans Alexsi Gorlinsky and Ivan Samchuck for participating in the funeral of our Fellow soldier - Joseph Polowsky."

"This is Joseph Polowsky. Thanks to him we could make contact quickly at the Elbe. He spoke German very well and could understand Russian. He was a translator and the soul of the meeting. He had time to be jolly or sympathetic anywhere and everywhere. Moreover, Sergeant Polowsky was my assistant," continued Albert. "And here is farmer Elijah Sams. I recognize Red Square. I saw it only in a movie. And here with the Kremlin behind them, stand office workers Fred Johnston and Bill Shiver."

"I see that you were able to show them many things. And here is engineer William Wells speaking with schoolchildren. He was drafted in the army for science and engineering. And here are businessmen Robert Haag, Murry Shulman, and Claude Moore. I wonder how they were able to come to the Soviet Union at the height of the 'Cold War'. As for that, I only remain envious of them."

Albert asked me what I had done since the war. I told him that I became a professor with a degree in technical sciences. I asked him how he had lived in the years after the war and what he had done.

Albert responded: "I continued to serve. The war was finished for me at the meeting on the Elbe. I continued to serve until the time came to retire. It's difficult to live on a pension. I didn't have a profession. At first, I worked as a clerk at one university. Then I decided it was necessary to become a professional. I began to study. I got an education in law. I'm working as a lawyer. I have a ranch and small piece of land in Texas. I grow vegetables and fruit. It's enough for our family. It's enough for you if you come as my guest. We invite you. It's very beautiful. I have four grandchildren. My son is a lieutenant colonel. He graduated from military college. However, he finished better than I and is working as an engineer. We have these soldiers who finish college well and go into the technical and engineering troops; those that are bad go in the infantry. I got in the infantry. Therefore, I was sent to study again after I was discharged," said Albert laughing.

"And you're not afraid of war?" I asked.

"No, we're not afraid. We know the Russians and believe that they don't want it either. They know what war is. Nobody lost so many people and had so much wasted in the war as you. My friends, neighbors, and fellow soldiers don't want war either, and I know that," continued Albert.

"And how then did you understand the declaration of your president about the necessity of increased nuclear potential and display?"

Albert answered with a smile. "We are already accustomed to it. All Americans make it their business and each makes it his occupation. Politicians on policy."

"It seems that it is a dangerous mistake of the Americans," I said. The decision to have or not have war is made by the president in the end. Therefore, the business of politics could be concluded with the danger of a military adventure. What do you think?"

"Ask me something easier", said Albert.

"Good," I answered. "Why do so few people in America know about your meeting with Gregori Goloborodko though it happened earlier? In the Soviet Union, it was published on the same day thanks to the operative carried by Alexander Ustinov. From you, I know that you left Trebsen with your reconnaissance patrol on the morning of April 25, 1945, and arrived in Torgau with the task of meeting the Russians. But some former American generals wrote in their memoirs that they had been sent to the Elbe and were waiting for those mysterious Russians for a long time."

(Ed. note: The original text contained material regarding the experiences of the American Generals - much of it was quotes from books by Bradley and Eisenhower.)

A. Olshansky continues:

"We don't see authors writing about the first meeting at Strehla. Why is nothing written about your meeting?"

Albert answered, "You asked about Bradley and Eisenhower. We thought about the possible meeting with the Russians at the end of April. I remember the hullabaloo that began after the announcement of Eisenhower's order that the Mulde and Elbe Rivers were the borders of the meeting of the allied troops with the advancing Soviet armies from the east. The aspiration to become a big part of history by being the first to establish contact with the Russians was a competition in resourcefulness for our American and other English and Canadian divisions because it was such an honor for us. Press and radio correspondents went like a swarm of worried bees from one group to another if a rumor of a possible meeting arose. And for all that, they missed the first meeting. Only your Ustinov was lucky. Now it is a well-known fact that the information about the first meeting of the allies was supposed to be published at the same time in Washington, London, and Moscow."

"That's why, when the command became known about the meeting of the two reconnaissance patrols of the American 69th Division with the advanced unit of

Soviet 58th Guards Infantry Divisions in the area of the two cities of Strehla and Torgau, the decision was made by the press to name the largest city which could be found in the area of the meeting. This was the city of Torgau. This accounts for the different interpretations in the press."

"The battle messages have been written so the affairs are in order and this is now in publications in Europe and America."

"In America, it is very important for a business to be first. It is important to be better. This accounts for the aspiration of our American writers to be first in everything. This is publicity. So this is what happened at the Elbe."

I told Albert that I had written an article in the "Red Star" about the meeting at the Elbe. They promised me it would be published the 25th of April in 1985, and they really did it. "I saw what was happening on our side 40 years ago and remember it well. However, at the moment of the meeting at the Elbe, I was with most of the soldiers of the reconnaissance patrol on a ridge beneath the city of Strehla on the morning of the 25th - and you were with Goloborodko. You were clarifying something on your maps and having a long talk about the trip to Kreinitz which we could see on the shore of the Elbe without a map. Then you sent two jeeps back. I found out later it was with a report. About what? It was about the wireless radio you had. After arriving in Kreinitz in the location of our regiment and after a festive meeting and dinner, you suddenly left us and went to the location of your troops."

Albert listened attentively to our translator and with the final words, began to laugh and said, "The connection for you, if you didn't know, was that the distance from our regiment to Strehla exceeded the capacity of our radio."

"Besides, to go from the location of our troops, I was supposed to get permission from our commander. An order had been given not to leave the limits of the five mile zone. All the more, I was supposed to know if I had the right to stay with my reconnaissance patrol in Kreinitz in the morning. At 17:00, Craig's patrol arrived in Kreinitz."

"The appearance of Major Craig made my task easier. The commander was worried because he didn't have any information from me. The plane sent to search for our patrol came back with nothing. They decided to send a search group. Major Craig was the leader. On the way to Strehla, he met two jeeps of my patrol and knew where he could find me right away in Kreinitz."

During one of the evenings, we met William Robertson who was a professor of neurosurgery in Los Angeles. Our tables were next to each other. I sat at one of them with our translator and Albert and his wife. William Robertson sat with his friends at the other one. We were so fascinated with the conversation and photographs that no one was aware of anything around them.

W. Robertson showed us his photographs and talked about a recent meeting with Alexander Silvashko. Robertson told us that Silvashko wasn't able to participate in the making of the movie at the Elbe because of family circumstances. And then English television invited him to go to Silvashko in Byelorussia. On the way to Silvashko's village of Kolki, he visited Moscow and Minsk. Alexander had tears in his eyes when he met Robertson. Silvashko showed him his Byelorussia where, at the age of 63, he was still working as the director of the village school. Silvashko was 23 years old at the time of the meeting on the destroyed bridge in Torgau.

The movie making came to an end. We separated, but were to be reunited at the Elbe on the 25th of April in 1985.

The future meeting with the American veterans who we had shaken hands with and hugged at the Elbe in April 1945, and with whom we were happily together in the victory at the enemy's border, caused mental anguish for the Soviet veterans. How would the meeting be? Would the "Spirit of the Elbe" be reflected? So many years had passed. Once more there would be a meeting - no longer as young soldiers and officers, but as gray-haired people with different laws and political persuasions.

But the first contacts became really sentimental friendships of mutual respect. They understood that the memory of the Elbe was alive.

Twenty-five Soviet veterans arrived in Leipzig, Germany, on April 24, 1985, with their leader, Colonel-General Yuri Naumenko. The same evening, American veterans who had arrived earlier invited the Soviet delegation to an organ concert in one of the old cathedrals in Leipzig. They were all very solemn and calm in the hall. Everyone observed each other. When the concert was over and all the people went to the street, loud exclamations and hugs began. They didn't have a translator around and were forced to explain themselves as they had 40 years before - with gestures and smiles. In the dark of the Leipzig night, there were joyous roars and laughing. Everybody was very glad about this meeting and filled with emotion anticipating the events of the next day.

On the 25th of April, buses were directed to Torgau. It was a cold, rainy day, not like spring. Along the road, people of all ages greeted the veterans with flowers and small flags.

Both groups of veterans were immediately directed to the shore of the Elbe to the obelisk on one of the sides of which, turned toward the river, were inscribed the words: "Here at the Elbe on April 25, 1945, the troops of the First Ukrainian Front of the Red Army got together with the American troops." Wreaths were lain at the obelisk. Hymns of the U.S.S.R., U.S.A., and G.D.R. were heard.

A rally commenced. From the platform, it was obvious that the squares and streets of Torgau were filled with people. These were people on the balconies of buildings and the roofs of houses and buses. And on the bridge over the Elbe, everyone saw columns of people with banners. In a city of about twenty thousand inhabitants, more than twenty-five thousand people gathered at the rally.

It seemed to everyone to be an appeal not to regret using force in the name of the preservation of peace. The rain destroyed the text which had been prepared for Yuri Naumenko. But he didn't need to look at it. He spoke about the same thing - that of suffering - for peace, which was new to all these people; about the sorrow of war, which should not happen to mankind again.

On this important day, we should solidly reaffirm with everyone that our common language is the language of friendship. We gave the oath at the Elbe in this language. It became sacred for the veterans of the Soviet Union and the U.S.A., and at every meeting we ask each other before all: "Do you remember this oath?" And we hear in response, "I remember. I do everything to have peace on earth."

A good speech on this spirit was given by American veteran William Beswick. There was a proposal to celebrate the 25th of April every year as "Elbe Day - A Day of Peace".

A reaffirmation of the "Oath at the Elbe" was read to the Soviet and American veterans:

"Oath at the Elbe"

by Soviet and American participants of the Elbe River link-up.1985

Reaffirmation

40th Anniversary of the Soviet-American Elbe Link-up 1985

We, Soviet and American war veterans, assembled here today, forty years after the historic link-up of the allied Soviet and American troops on the Elbe River, once again reaffirm our allegiance to the <u>pledge</u> made by our comrades-in-arms on April 25, 1945, <u>to dedicate our lives to furthering friendship between the peoples of the USSR and USA so that wars never again happen.</u>

The attempt of the Nazis to ensure their world domination cost mankind during World War II fifty million lives. Reminding the world about this grim lesson of history today, when world tensions have reached a dangerous level, we once again resolutely come out for securing the first and foremost human right of all nations — to live in peace; for a cessation of the arms race; and the prevention of war which can destroy human civilization.

True to the spirit of the Elbe, we firmly believe in the following:

- that we honor our dead.
- that we renew and reaffirm our friendship.
- that the friendship of the Elbe shall be everlasting.
- that we work toward a better understanding and reduction of tension between our two nations.
- that we strive toward a reduction of both conventional and nuclear arms.
- that we diligently dedicate ourselves toward mutual respect between nations.
- that we must work diligently toward maintaining peace between our two nations and all other nations of the world.

Today there is no alternative but to live in peace! Therefore we, American and Soviet war veterans in memory of those perished in the battlefields of The War, and those who are no more, and on behalf of their descendants, urge today all honest people to spare no effort to avert war!

YES — to friendly meetings and talks to solve all
disputable issues.
NO — to war!

Torgau, the G.D.R.

In confirmation of these words, hundreds of white doves were released and flew over the Elbe. The rally was over. Veterans Charles Forrester, Ivan Samchuck, and Alexei Gorlinsky shook hands with each other and Ted Polowsky, the son of Joseph, joined in. It was a handshake of people of different generations, like the oath of the fathers given to the sons.

It was raining. We rested silently at the embankment, staring at the Elbe. We have that to remember.

On the same day in Torgau, a wreath was laid on the common grave of the Soviet soldiers who died in 1945. Then the American and Soviet participants of the meeting at the Elbe went to the town cemetery to honor the memory of their friend Joseph Polowsky. He was an average American who worked many years as a taxi driver in Chicago. In the middle of 1983, he sent the community of Soviet veterans a very unusual letter. He wrote very bravely that he was terminally ill. When he knew the decision of the doctors, he said good-bye to his Soviet friends and said that he put in his will to be buried in the same place in Torgau where he met with the Soviet soldiers. He asked to have two hands clasped in a strong handshake on his monument.

Making his will to be buried in Torgau, Joseph Polowsky wanted to prove that the spirit of collaboration which was born in the fight with fascism would remain forever in the memory of the American people.

In the fall of 1983, when we got the sad news about the death of Joseph, Ivan Samchuck and Alexei Gorlinsky went from the Soviet Union to Torgau to bury their friend.

The next day in Torgau, April 26, 1985, an international press conference took place.

We were surprised at the first question:

Where exactly was the first meeting – in Torgau or Strehla – and was the text of the oath put in writing?

The leader of the press conference said that a participant of the first meeting – Alexander Olshansky – was seated in the hall and could answer the question.

The first meeting of the American patrol of former Lieutenant Albert Kotzebue and the commander of the regiment of our division, Gregori Goloborodko, took place in the morning of April 25, 1945, on a ridge below the city of Strehla. There was no correspondent and very few people know about it. At 13:00, the patrol crossed the Elbe River and arrived in the village of Kreinitz at the headquarters of the 175th Guards Regiment where A. Kotzebue reported to the commander of the regiment, Lieutenant-Colonel Gordeyev, about his arrival for building a liaison with the troops of the Red Army.

Several people participated in this meeting; correspondents Alexander Ustinov, Konstantin Simonov, Alexander Krivitsky, Gregori Homzor and others. Pictures of this meeting were published in newspapers and journals.

In March of 1985, I, together with A. Kotzebue, was in the same place and participated in the movie, "Yanks Meet Reds", shot by English television. I, as a communication specialist, only knew on April 26, 1945, that the 173rd Regiment of our machine-gunners under Second Lieutenant Alexander Silvashko met with the patrol of Lieutenant William Robertson.

The only difference was that A. Kotzebue came to the location of our 175th

Regiment and W. Robertson took away officers of the 173rd Regiment to his 273rd Regiment and then to the headquarters of the 69th Infantry Division.

Both meetings took place the very same day in the very same divisions. The difference in time was very little.

But the first meeting in Strehla, thanks to correspondent Alexander Ustinov of the newspaper "Pravda", was published in the journal "Ogonek" ("Fire"), and the next meeting in Torgau was published in the American journal "Life". How matters stood in Torgau can be told by Robertson and Silvashko, who are present in the hall.

The G.D.R. correspondent repeated his question, "And do you have a written text of the oath?"

I continued my answer.

The oath during the meeting in Strehla and Kreinitz was, of course, oral. And the first to write about it was Joseph Polowsky. Some Soviet veterans familiar with the oath are Gergori Goloborodko, Alexander Gordeyev, Alexei Baranov, Leonid Volodarsky, Gregori Prokopyev, Peter Alekseev, Alexander Afanasev, Alexei Gorlinsky, Ivan Samchuck, me, and many others. Some of the American veterans familiar with it are Charles Forrester, William Wells, Elijah Sams, Fred Johnston, Bill Shiver, Robert Haag, Murry Schulman, Claude Moore, Peter Setnek, Bill Beswick, and others.

However, we didn't know that fate would put us in this historic event. We were soldiers and not diplomats and the text wasn't put into writing.

More information about what happened to Major Larionov and Captain Nyeda following the link-up is described in the following text. These details were reported in a document which was obtained from A. Silvashko by the Torgau Kulturhaus to be included in this book. The document was prepared by Vladimir Demyanenko, a member of the Journalist's Association of the Ukraine. V. Demyanenko's signature on the document was authenticated by O.S. Mikitjuk, Director of the Ministry of the Creative Center, City of Browar Serviceseals.

The document was prefaced: Published and compiled from a book about the April 1945 meeting at the Elbe of the soldiers of the armies of the allied countries - members of the anti-Hitler coalition.

V. Demyanenko wrote that Nyeda's wife told him about her husband's fate:

It is difficult to put into words the feelings which were experienced by the officers and soldiers of the 173rd Infantry Regiment at the April 25th meeting with the American reconnaissance patrol of Lieutenant W. Robertson. The allies invited our soldiers to visit the headquarters of the 69th American Division. Battalion Commander V. P. Nyeda did not have the right to permit such a friendly visit. And only with the arrival of the unit's assistant commander, Major Larionov, did a few soldiers and officers go to the allies. Larionov and Nyeda were included in this group.

The superiors of the command reacted negatively to this incident. Soon Major Larionov and Captain Nyeda were expelled from the party and dismissed from their jobs. Vasili Petrovich was sent to the army's reserves. Receiving neither an increase in rank nor allied awards, he was discharged from the reserves in 1946.

Major Larionov was not able to bear the heavy moral blow; he went into the hospital on account of mental stress and died suddenly.

Until retirement, V. P. Nyeda worked as an electrician. He died in 1991.

A. Olshansky wrote that Major Larionov and Captain Nyeda were eliminated from the party, punished and ordered to be disciplined. They were discharged from the army after the war. In May of 1945, the journal "Ogonek" ("Fire") and the newspapers reported only about the reconnaissance patrols of A. Kotzebue and G. Golobodko and so it continued for 30 years.

Excerpts from information and a 1994 article provided by A. Olshansky illustrate the feelings many veterans share:

"Bridges That Unite"

It seems that was only yesterday. The Elbe, the bridges and the ferry crossings, the Russian and American soldiers running to meet each other... In any case, we participants of those memorable events of 1945 have arrived regularly in Torgau for 49 years and count meeting allies at the Elbe as one of the main events in our lives.

Embraces, memoirs, tears, the front-line losses of friends and those who were like brothers - the years go on - tales and, again, tears. In the next Elbe Days-'94, it seems that veterans from all ends of the earth and all the western groups of troops are in this small, cozy city. It's a warm, sunny day. All the inhabitants of Torgau are in the streets and at the waterfronts of the Elbe.

The main task for our veterans is to pass the Spirit of the Elbe, peace and friendship, to our young people, children and grandchildren. This is a difficult task, but we expect to have time while we are alive. We'd like to mark the 50th Anniversary of the victory and meeting at the Elbe by building a memorial park on the waterfront of the Elbe in the city of Strehla with the joint efforts of the countries of Russia, the U.S.A. and Germany. This will be an example of the completed creation of a single structure of the meetings at the Elbe by the allied troops from Torgau to Muhlburg, Kreinitz, Strehla and Sitzheim. Not only did the meeting of the allies take place in this region, but also of the freed prisoners-of-war from the camps.

- - - -

The bridges over the Elbe were restored after the war. Bridges are a symbol of the allied "European meetings" - a symbol for the union of nations for the common cause of peace. **Bridges - they are examples of understanding and of the desire to meet and know each other better. Let us have as many as possible in our lives.**

Grigori Goloborodko: born in 1912; died in 1958; Lieutenant of the Soviet Army during World War II; following the war, worked as machine operator on a collective farm in his native Ukrainian village of Salovka.

Alexander T. Gordeyev: Finished World War II as a Commander of the Guards 175th Regiment; born August 25, 1916; participant of the meeting at the Elbe; retired from the Army in 1962 as a partially-disabled veteran.

Alexander V. Olshansky: Major-General; born in 1925; Professor, Doctor of Technical Sciences; Institute of Railway Transport Engineering, Moscow; Honorary Citizen of Dallas, Texas, and the state of Kansas.

Gregory S. Prokopyev: Retired Captain; born November 25, 1923; Former Company Commander in the 58th Guards Division; participant of the meeting at the Elbe; Honorary Citizen of Dallas, Texas, and the state of Kansas.

Leonid V. Volodarsky: Retired Colonel of the 130th Artillery, 58th Guards Division; born June 25, 1924; wounded at the Elbe; ended the war as a First Lieutenant.

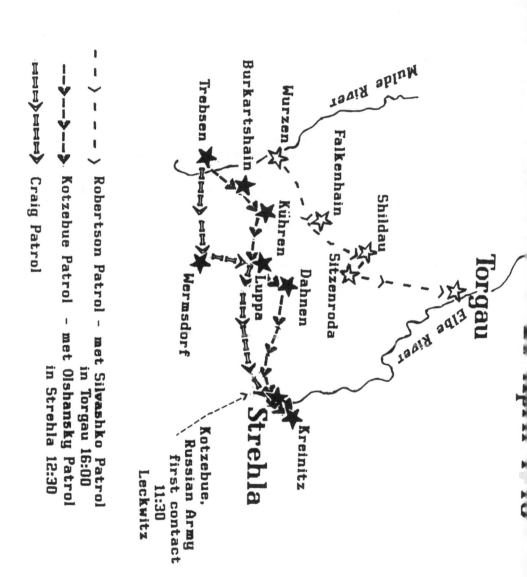

- - - - →   Robertson Patrol - met Silvashko Patrol
              in Torgau 16:00

- ▼ - ▼ - →   Kotzebue Patrol - met Olshansky Patrol
              in Strehla 12:30

▦▦▦▦▷   Craig Patrol

HANDS ACROSS THE ELBE INDEX